THE CHAMPIONSHIPS
WIMBLEDON
Official Annual 2001

JOHN PARSONS

Photographs by
CLIVE BRUNSKILL, GARY M. PRIOR and **ALEX LIVESEY**
of Allsport/Getty Images

RICHARD POULTER

Editor
JOHN PARSONS

Production Manager
STEVEN PALMER

Publishing Development Manager
SIMON SANDERSON

Art Editor
STEVE SMALL

Managing Editor
ROBERT YARHAM

Publicity and promotion
ANNALISA ZANELLA

Marketing and New Media Manager
NICK POULTER

Photography
CLIVE BRUNSKILL
GARY M. PRIOR
ALEX LIVESEY

Photo Research, Allsport
ELAINE LOBO
ANDY SMITH

This first edition published in 2001 by Hazleton Publishing Ltd,
3 Richmond Hill, Richmond, Surrey TW10 6RE

Hazleton Publishing Ltd is a member of Profile Media Group Plc

ISBN: 1-903135-01-X

Printed in England by Bath Press Ltd

Colour reproduction by Barrett Berkeley Ltd, London

Results tables are reproduced by courtesy of
The All England Lawn Tennis Club

This book is produced with the assistance of Rolex

ROLEX

FOREWORD

By common consent Wimbledon 2001 will be remembered as one of the best ever.

The 115th Championships began with the demise of the top-seeded Martina Hingis and climaxed 14 days later with extraordinary scenes on Centre Court as Goran Ivanisevic (a wild card ranked 125 in the world) at last triumphed in a Wimbledon final (his fourth) by edging out Pat Rafter 9-7 in the fifth set of a titanic contest. This match exemplified sport at its best. Two very popular athletes playing outstanding tennis in front of a committed capacity crowd which had brought inflatable kangaroos, Croatian flags and other such essentials for the occasion.

In the ladies' singles, Jennifer Capriati, who had won the first two legs of a potential Grand Slam, was eclipsed in the semi-final by the 19-year-old Belgian Justine Henin who became a heroine at home. In the final, Venus Williams proved to be too powerful and defended her title successfully 6-0 in the final set.

During Wimbledon fortnight we were blessed with glorious weather until the final few days. On the second Saturday only 51 minutes' play was possible so fans had to make do with an entertaining live interview on Centre Court with former U.S. president Bill Clinton who gave his reflection on his own game — 'aggressive and inaccurate' — and on Wimbledon: 'The greatest tournament in the world.'

Record attendances were the norm this year with the largest crowds ever on eight of the first nine days as The Championships benefited from the major new facilities created under the All England Club's long-term plan. Overall, 490,081 came to Wimbledon this year — over 33,000 more than the previous highest total. The Aorangi Park amphitheatre with its widescreen situated alongside the new No. 1 Court was so successful that, on the Thursday night of the second week, another big screen was erected at the southern end of the grounds so that more spectators could share the excitement.

2001 will be remembered as the year when Tim Henman reached his third Wimbledon semi-final, playing some of his best tennis before Goran Ivanisevic got the better of him in an interrupted match spread over three days. It was also the year in which the new faces really made an impact: Juan Carlos Ferrero, Lleyton Hewitt, Andy Roddick, Roger Federer, Taylor Dent, Justine Henin, Kim Clijsters, Jelena Dokic and a host of young players from Eastern Europe.

I very much hope you will enjoy this record of all the drama of Wimbledon 2001.

Tim Phillips

Tim Phillips
Chairman of The All England Lawn Tennis & Croquet Club
and the Committee of Management of The Championships

Goran Ivanisevic and
the Wimbledon trophy.

INTRODUCTION

EW were in any doubt as to the two most intriguing questions which were going to be answered during Wimbledon 2001. Could Pete Sampras maintain that air of invincibility which had helped to win the men's singles a phenomenal record seven times in eight years, despite a record coming into The Championships which was his weakest for almost a decade? And could Jennifer Capriati, who had already won the Australian Open in January and the French Open at Roland Garros two weeks earlier, take another major step along the road to what would be the first women's Grand Slam since Steffi Graf in 1988?

Events during the famous fortnight would not only provide the answers to those two questions but a host of others, not least how well two of the leading contenders, Andre Agassi, desperately anxious to regain the title he originally won in 1992, and Venus Williams, the defending ladies' singles champion, would bounce back after their unexpected setbacks in Paris.

Most observers seemed to agree that there were six best-equipped challengers for the men's singles — Pete Sampras, Andre Agassi, Lleyton Hewitt, Pat Rafter, Yevgeny Kafelnikov and Britain's Tim Henman — plus five among the ladies — Jennifer Capriati, Venus Williams, her sister Serena, top-seeded Martina Hingis and former champion, Lindsay Davenport, although the latter had hardly played for the previous three months through injury.

Equally there were a host of other names which could be in contention or were just beginning to be recognised by the public. Among them, of course, were Greg Rusedski with his thunderbolt serves, Marat Safin the U.S. Open champion, Andy Roddick, the sparky new American kid on the block and Roger Federer, the 19-year-old Swiss player with so much to offer. Another player who the crowds would be happy to see again, even though no one, not even he, thought it would be such a prolonged visit, was Goran Ivanisevic. Most assumed the Croat had been given a wild card as a sympathy vote for a three-times runner-up struggling with fitness and confidence, rather than as a serious pace-maker. How gloriously wrong could we be!

There were also the outstanding Belgian girls, Kim Clijsters and Justine Henin to look out for, plus Jelena Dokic and a host of attractive and entertaining young Russians ready to upset rankings in the ladies' singles, who would help to compensate for the absence through prolonged injuries of Anna Kournikova and Mary Pierce.

A third issue was also relevant. What impact, if any, would the new seeding system have? Seedings for The Championships have invariably been a topic for argument and debate ever since they were first introduced in 1927, though never more so than during the build-up this time. The controversy actually began a few days before the start of the previous year's event, when Spanish players, Alex Corretja and Albert Costa, who had been dropped from a seeded position in favour of other players with infinitely superior grass-court credentials, boycotted the tournament. They felt that because a new ATP rule, introduced that year, meant their ranking would suffer if they did not compete, then it was only fair that their world ranking should be respected in their seedings.

The committee of the All England Club, in seeking a solution which would be fair to the tournament, the public and the clay-courters, decided that, instead of a seeding committee, the seedings for the men's singles would be decided by a computer programmed to give added weight to grass-court performances.

The players were still not happy even though the whole principle of seeding was to produce a balanced draw for the general good of the game. Apart from other factors, they did not seem able to appreciate and that after two months of clay-court tournaments the world rankings had obviously been distorted in their favour. Nor did they seem impressed by the illuminating fact that Wimbledon's seeding success rate in predicting the four semi-finalists over the previous ten years was superior to those at the three other Grand Slam tournaments: Wimbledon had a 52 per cent success rate, Roland Garros, the other most specialised clay-court surface, a mere 18 per cent, and the Australian and U.S. Opens 50 per cent.

In the end, after much painstaking negotiations by the chairman of the All England Club, Tim Phillips, who spoke personally to many of the leading players, a compromise was reached. Starting with the 2001 Championships, not just Wimbledon but all four Slams would increase the number of seeds from 16 to 32 and use a formula which combined ATP ranking points with the best results by the players on that particular surface on a graded scale, over the three previous years.

Three players still withdrew. All cited injuries, including the French Open champion, Gustavo Kuerten, who had been a fervent critic of the old seeding system. They were to miss being part of one of the most exciting and most memorable stagings of The Championships, about to unfold.

Wimbledon 25 June - 8 July 2001

Founded in 1877, Wimbledon is both the oldest and most prestigious tournament in the world of tennis. A veritable shrine to the sport, it is also the last Grand Slam competition still played on grass. Indeed, to ensure the grass is in peak condition, Wimbledon's two main show courts are left empty except for two weeks each year.

www.rolex.com

"Keep off the grass." Only top seeds allowed.

Perpetual Spirit

Rolex Lady-Datejust and Rolex Datejust. Officially Certified Swiss Chronometers.

ROLEX

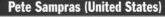

Pete Sampras (United States)
Age: 29
Born: Washington DC
World ranking: 6

ALTHOUGH without a tournament win since Wimbledon 2000, when he not only broke Roy Emerson's record of winning 12 men's singles titles in Grand Slams but also equalled Bjorn Borg's achievement of winning at least one Grand Slam for eight consecutive years, few questioned the decision to name the American as top seed.

Time and again over the years an aura had seemed to inspire and protect Sampras on the grass courts of Wimbledon which he had come to love so much. But could it last for another year?

Most of his fellow players believed it could although for the first time in a decade he went into the tournament knowing there was much work to be done. The impressive variety of attacking serves were still there but perhaps not quite the instinctive anticipation and speed of response before those attacking forehands which had so often been a decisive second shot.

'I know the year has been disappointing so far but I'm sure that at Wimbledon I can soon turn things round' he insisted.

Twelve months on, despite being limited in his matchplay by injuries in the early part of the year, he was the overwhelming favourite not only to establish that record as his own but to equal Bjorn Borg's achievement as the only man to win at least one Grand Slam title in eight consecutive years.

Sampras's many skills, principally his wonderful ability to vary an array of winning serves, his attacking forehands and those spectacular 'slam dunks', have seldom been more effectively demonstrated than on the immaculate lawns of the All England Club.

At the same time Sampras, who was accompanied at The Championships by his American actress wife Bridgette Wilson, was well aware of how every year the task gets tougher.

Andre Agassi (United States)
Age: 31
Born: Las Vegas, Nevada
World ranking: 2

LIKE Pete Sampras, Agassi arrived at The Championships with a reputation to restore, rather than to prove, following some disappointing results after a brilliant start to the year when he successfully defended the Australian Open title and then won the first two Tennis Masters Series events in 2001 at Indian Wells and Key Biscayne.

In his mind, though, he arrived fitter, smarter and playing a higher level of tennis than when he won the title in 1992, saying 'I think it's about time I won Wimbledon again and if I am going to win another Slam this is the one I think it is most likely to be.'

Still one of the finest returners in the game, Agassi was hoping that the way the courts at the All England Club had become firmer over the years, offering a slightly higher bounce, would suit his game and provide him with added encouragement.

His long-standing relationship with former ladies' singles champion, Steffi Graf, meant there was no sign of media interest in their private lives diminishing.

3

Pat Rafter (Australia)
Age: 28
Born: Mount Isa, Queensland
World ranking: 10

HAVING finished runner-up in the previous year's final, Rafter was certainly the seed winning the most sentimental support. A true sportsman, he had charmed crowds with his attacking skills, athleticism and personality for years and although he was not committing himself, many felt that this could be his last attempt at winning Wimbledon.

A history of injuries was almost certainly one of the main reasons why he had been unable to add to the U.S. Open titles he won in successive years, 1997–8. Following surgery to repair a rotator cuff in his right shoulder in October 1999, he recovered well enough to reach the Wimbledon final and lead Australia into the Davis Cup final the following year.

Rafter, a 6ft 1in, ever-amiable right-hander, is the third youngest in a family of nine children and his appreciation of family life is reflected in the enormous amount of charity work he, like many other players, undertakes for terminally ill and under-privileged children.

A natural serve-and-volleyer, with a game ideally suited to grass, he was confident that this could be his Wimbledon year.

Marat Safin (Russia)
Age: 21
Born: Moscow
World ranking: 3

4

THE previous September when he outplayed Pete Sampras to win the U.S. Open title, Marat Safin looked capable of conquering the tennis world — but with reservations. For too often with the strapping 6ft 4in right-hander, who played most of his grass-roots junior tennis on the red clay courts in Spain, it is a case of all or nothing.

When he is in the right mood his tennis can be awesome. When things start to go wrong, the head drops and his confidence can evaporate with damaging haste, which is why, even before he suffered a muscle strain on his left side in Dubai in February, the inconsistent days had returned.

In an attempt to bring some maturity to his game, Safin hired Mats Wilander, the former Australian, French Open and U.S. Open champion as his coach. 'I wouldn't have taken the job if I didn't think he had the ability to reach the very top' said the Swede, who himself was meticulously efficient as a player.

Safin certainly has a serve which can cause damage on grass and an improving volley but still had to show that he really believed he could play on the surface. For many Europeans that is easier said than done.

Lleyton Hewitt (Australia)
Age: 20
Born: Adelaide
World ranking: 5

SO far in two previous visits, the often noisily energetic Hewitt had not gone beyond the third round and in 2000 he was unexpectedly beaten in the first round by unseeded Jan-Michael Gambill.

However, having won the Stella Artois title at Queen's Club for a second successive year, two weeks before The Championships, again beating Pete Sampras along the way and then Tim Henman in the final, he certainly looked a reasonable outside prospect.

The slim, hard-working and supremely fit Australian has a reasonable record on all surfaces but despite his Queen's Club success, knew that he would need to come and volley more if he was to duplicate that success at Wimbledon.

Mentally durable enough to reach the top, he is also one of the quickest players about the court but on grass, in particular, needs to broaden his range of winners and be able to force errors from his opponents earlier, rather than allowing so many points to become mini endurance tests. A quick learner but perhaps not quite ready to win the title just yet.

Tim Henman (Great Britain)
Age: 26
Born: Oxford
World ranking: 11

MANY felt that this year might present Britain's most talented singles player for more than 60 years with the chance to provide the home nation with its first men's champion since the late Fred Perry in 1936.

Despite his disappointing record in the three other Grand Slams, never going beyond the fourth round, Henman had consistently produced much of his best form at Wimbledon in recent years, being a quarter finalist twice and a semi-finalist twice since 1996.

The British number one, who had been in or around the world's top ten for five years, remained full of praise for long-serving coach, David Felgate, from whom he had parted company earlier in the year but was also convinced that being made to think more himself was proving good for him and his game.

He was not alone in hoping that the improved results he had enjoyed on clay in Europe in the weeks building up to The Championships, not least reaching the quarter finals in Monte Carlo — plus the dedicated fitness training routine he had been following — would be rewarded at the right time and at the right place.

Yevgeny Kafelnikov (Russia)
Age: 27
Born: Sochi
World ranking: 6

FROM the moment he first made his mark on the men's tour in a major way in 1994, many have felt that Kafelnikov was one of those rare players with the ability to capture all four of the Grand Slam titles. All too often, however, his patience snaps, the control and commitment disappear and he loses to opponents one would expect him to have beaten.

That had been particularly so at Wimbledon, where he has never made it beyond the last eight and that was only once, way back in 1995. Despite winning the French Open in 1996 and the Australian Open in 1999, on his way to becoming world number one, there are times when there is on ominous lack of self-belief running through his veins.

In 2000 it began to look as if he might be putting those problems behind him when he won the gold medal in the singles at the Olympic Games and became a national hero. Yet after reaching the semi-finals at Indian Wells, where he was beaten by Pete Sampras, he won only two of his next nine matches, prompting coach Larry Stefanki to quit in frustration. He clearly has the ability to win Wimbledon but not, it seems, the temperament.

Juan Carlos Ferrero (Spain)
Age: 21
Born: Onteniente
World ranking: 4

THIS was a journey into the unknown for the Spaniard, nicknamed 'Mosquito' because of his slim physique which belies the enormous amount of mental and physical stamina within. Apart from one or two matches as a junior, this was to be his first serious experience on grass.

Yet despite the way he had joked about the prospect during his outstanding clay-court season which included titles in Estoril, Barcelona and Rome, plus a runners-up place in Hamburg when the fatigue of so many matches in such a short space of time caught up with him, one felt that deep down it was a challenge which became all the more appealing, the more he thought about it.

A wonderful stylist, able and willing to hit elegant groundstrokes from the back of the court all day, Ferrero had considerably improved his first serve in the first half of the year and on the rare occasions he was encouraged to do so, had showed that he could also put away volleys with pace and precision. It was a debut awaited with great interest.

ALTHOUGH still on top of the world rankings, Hingis arrived at Wimbledon not having added to her total of five Grand Slam titles since the Australian Open in January 1999 and with growing concern about her ability to counter the power which now increasingly seems to be the dominant factor on the Sanex WTA Tour.

Her only success at The Championships was in 1997 although in 200? the quarter final she lost against the eventual champion, Venus William? was rated as the most exciting ladies' match of the fortnight.

As in 1999, her relationship with her mother and coach, Melanie Mol? tor, was proving difficult to maintain. They had parted company aga? after Hingis's run of reaching ten consecutive finals came to an end at I? dian Wells and she also struggled to impose herself in the expected sty? in Key Biscayne.

Mother and daughter had been re-united in time for the French Op? where Hingis reached the semi-finals, and was beaten by Jennifer Capria? but somehow the enthusiasm and zest were not quite the same.

Martina Hingis (Switzerland)
Age: 20
Born: Kosice, Slovakia
World ranking: 1

Venus Williams (United States)
Age: 21
Born: Lynwood, California
World ranking: 2

DESPITE a stunning first-round defeat by Barbara Schett at the French Open, which left her relatively short of match practice going into The Championships, the tall, fierce-hitting American was still the favourite with the main tennis public, if not all the bookmakers, to successfully defend her title. The general feeling was that although she might beat herself, no one was really likely to beat her.

Constantly improving, she had shown earlier in the year her ability to lift her powerful, athletic game whenever forced to do so. Her serve is probably as good as any there has ever been in women's tennis and on grass that asset would be even more significant.

After Wimbledon 2000, when she brought her game to a new peak in the final against Lindsay Davenport, she went on to win the U.S. Open and Olympic gold. This year after being beaten dramatically 6-1 6-1 by Martina Hingis in the semi-finals of the Australian Open, she took a break before returning looking even fitter and stronger, to win in Key Biscayne and Hamburg.

Lindsay Davenport (United States)
Age: 25
Born: Palos Verdes, California
World ranking: 3

DAVENPORT twice reached the semi-finals before her powerful though sometimes erratic game came together perfectly when she beat the about-to-retire Steffi Graf in the 1999 final. Even so she was unable to fend off the even more impressive challenge she found herself facing from Venus Williams 12 months later.

By her standards the first half of 2001 had been disappointing but that could largely be put down to a knee injury which had kept her off court for almost three months. She came into The Championships uplifted more by the way she came through the week without further trouble from the knee, rather than her victory on her return to the tour at Eastbourne. The field had been low-key, with only one other competitor from the top ten.

On her day Davenport has often demonstrated that by making full use of her serve, her height and her reach, she can play irresistible tennis. At the same time her naturally aggressive, often risky game can sometimes leave dangerously little room for error.

Jennifer Capriati (United States)
Age: 25
Born: Wesley Chapel, Florida
World ranking: 4

IT was 11 years since Jennifer Capriati became the youngest player to be seeded at a Grand Slam tournament and the youngest to win a match at Wimbledon, when she was 14. Not content with that, a year later she became the youngest semi-finalist in the ladies' singles at Wimbledon when she beat Martina Navratilova in the quarter finals, inflicting her earliest Wimbledon defeat in 15 years.

Since then the continuing rise, the equally dramatic fall and then the return to fame and glory have been so well documented that a tearful Capriati at one point begged the media not to ask her about her past again but to concentrate on what she called 'the here and now and the future.'

Happily there has been much to tell. Indeed Capriati's victories at both the Australian and French Open tournaments earlier in the year meant that she arrived at Wimbledon half way to becoming the first player since Steffi Graf in 1988 to achieve the Grand Slam. Was it asking too much or could she keep the dream alive?

5

Serena Williams (United States)
Age: 19
Born: Saginaw, Michigan
World ranking: 5

BY no means had it been her best season so far. Her only tournament success earlier in the year had been at Indian Wells, where the last-minute withdrawal of Venus, citing injury, when the sisters should have played one another in the semi-finals, led to crowd protests against both girls and their father, Richard, during the final.

At Wimbledon 2000, Serena looked more likely to win the title than Venus until she seemed to freeze when they met in the semi-finals. The greatest moment of Serena's career had been at the U.S. Open in 1999 when she beat Martina Hingis in the final but admitted that Venus had gone a long way to helping her by pushing the Swiss player to the limit in a classic semi-final.

Sometimes she is not helped by having a bulkier frame than her older sister which at times limited her speed about the court. Her forehand, while powerful enough, sometimes lacked the control and accuracy for her to benefit from her naturally aggressive approach.

Amelie Mauresmo (France)
Age: 21
Born: Laye
World ranking: 6

EVER since she reached the final of the Australian Open in 1999 with a series of stunning performances, the tennis world had been expecting the tall, supremely fit and sturdily athletic Mauresmo to reproduce such form at the other Grand Slams.

They were still waiting, and a devastating first-round defeat at the French Open — where the pressure of being expected by the home crowd to repeat the success of the now-injured Mary Pierce, one year earlier, proved too much for her — was not going to help her.

Although possessing an effective enough serve and volley to thrive on the grass at Wimbledon, her past record at The Championships — one match won on her two previous visits, coupled with reports that she had pulled out of Eastbourne because she realised her confidence was so low — was hardly encouraging.

Suddenly her pre-Roland Garros form and belief, which had led to her winning two indoor titles, followed by the German Open and reaching the final of the Italian Open, had evaporated. The bookmakers were listing her at 25-1.

ALTHOUGH she had reached the fourth round at Wimbledon as a 16-year-old and had achieved a growing number of surprise victories without quite breaking through at the top level in the intervening years, the attacking, hard-hitting Clijsters was certainly one to watch.

Only two weeks before she had been within two points of winning a Grand Slam when she narrowly lost an epic French Open final against Jennifer Capriati. The final set, which Capriati won 12-10 was a memorable climax to the whole Paris fortnight.

Whether Clijsters could emulate that form on grass provoked contrasting views. Some felt that with her big serve and eager ability to volley she would present a threat to anyone. Others were not convinced that she moved well enough when kept under pressure. Clijsters, herself, was confident that the grass would pose her no more problems than any other surface and knew time was on her side. Like her boyfriend, Lleyton Hewitt, she was quite happy learning the tennis trade one step at a time.

Kim Clijsters (Belgium)
Age: 18
Born: Bilzen
World ranking: 7

Justine Henin (Belgium)
Age: 19
Born: Liège
World ranking: 9

AS former champion, Chris Evert, observed after watching her closely for the first time in Paris, 'Justine makes you reconsider the belief that these days you have to be big and powerful to succeed in women's tennis.' At barely 5ft 6in and weighing only 126 lb, she is certainly overshadowed physically by many of her opponents.

Yet in the 12 months between Wimbledon 2000 and 2001, enough powerful punches were packed into that light frame to lift her 100 places in the world rankings. On top of that the tennis world had discovered that she has a backhand which was already a match-winning joy to behold and a forehand which was rapidly becoming just as effective.

Her extraordinary lapse against Clijsters in the semi-finals of the French Open when she lost after leading by a set and 4-2, suggested that perhaps she might not have the temperament for the biggest occasions. Henin was aghast at such a suggestion and immediately promised 'I'll never let that happen again.' That same fighting mood is reflected in her resilient tennis.

THE CHAMPIONSHIPS WIMBLEDON

MONDAY 25 JUNE

day1

THE CHAMPIONSHIPS WIMBLEDON

ORDER OF PLAY

MONDAY 25th JUNE

2001

day 1 • sampras v clavet

Francisco Clavet (above) put his heart and soul into his first-round match but still had to bow to Pete Sampras (right), who had maintained the tradition of the defending men's singles champion opening the Centre Court programme on the first day.

The sun shone without a break on a record first-day crowd of 39,330, highlighting the multitude of colours among the thousands of flowers in full bloom. The unblemished, emerald courts looked better than ever and throughout the fortnight were to play better than ever. It was no wonder that Wimbledon was once called 'that little piece of tennis heaven in SW 19.'

For the players in the top half of the men's singles draw and the bottom half of the ladies' singles, it was a time to dream — some like Pete Sampras, of adding to already record success, others, such as Britain's Tim Henman in particular, of achieving a lifetime's ambition; Goran Ivanisevic simply of trying to show he justified his wild card.

That trio all advanced though Sampras had to work harder than some had expected to prevent Spain's Francisco Clavet causing more concern about whether the American's reign might at last be difficult to sustain. 'So far as I'm concerned he's still the King of Wimbledon, still the king of grass' said Clavet. 'When his serve works [which it did with encouraging regularity when there were signs of concern] then he works.'

Sampras, who reacted to suggestions that his form might be waning with just a hint of frustration, said 'I've been through this before but I can turn that around very quickly. I feel I have a pretty good chance.'

Inevitably, by the time the final matches on a thrilling Day One were finishing, half those who had been competing were left to dream only of another day. Five men and four ladies, who had been seeded to reach at least the last 32, were among the day's casualties. Seven among the nine had been beneficiaries of the decision to extend the number of singles seeds from 16 to 32.

Below: A perfect start to the fortnight in every respect as record crowds packed the viewing areas round Courts 3, 4 and 5.

The two exceptions were Jan-Michael Gambill, 12th seed among the men, who, one year after upsetting the then seventh-seeded Australian Lleyton Hewitt on the first round, was knocked out in five sets by fellow American Davis Cup player, Chris Woodruff, and, most remarkably of all, top-seeded Martina Hingis.

The growing cracks which Hingis had been striving to mask in her game since winning the last of her five Grand Slam titles at the Australian Open in January 1999, split wide open as she floundered and she was beaten 6-4 6-2 by the 83rd-ranked Spaniard, Virginia Ruano Pascual.

Once she lost her serve for the first time, largely through three double faults in the fifth game, an uninspired, increasingly worried world number one, was beaten comprehensively in 67 minutes. It was as if her 1999 nightmare when she lost to the then 16-year-old Jelena Dokic on the same court, had come back to haunt her.

It also meant that she became the first top seed in either the men's or ladies' singles to lose in the first round a second time. Including this upset, it was only the fifth time such a disaster had befallen the top seed since seedings were first introduced in 1927.

Given the previous credibility of the others who had suffered that fate — defending champion, Manuel Santana against Charlie Pasarell in 1967, Margaret Court against Billie Jean Moffitt (King) in 1962 and Lori McNeil against Steffi Graf in 1964 — this was probably the biggest upset of them all.

The explanation the first time it happened to Hingis was that it was largely emotional. It happened only two weeks after her distress at the French Open when she had to be dragged back in tears for the presentation ceremony, following her extravagant protest against a line call as she was beaten by Steffi Graf in the final, provoking a storm of booing from the crowd.

This time, she insisted, it should be blamed on a mild attack of tendinitis in her lower back which meant 'I was more or less only able to play from a standing position. I was afraid of moving because I didn't know exactly how far can I go and against any player these days you have to be able to run.'

For much of the match Hingis, who was reported to have practised for at least four hours a day in the time leading into The Championships, disguised the trouble well enough, though her volleys became so tentative and her groundstrokes so lacking in penetration that as the time progressed, one felt that, even allowing for the way her form had slid earlier in the year, something else had to be wrong.

It was unfortunate that the natural sympathy there would be for a player incapacitated in such circumstances, was diluted by her astonishing admission that she would probably have withdrawn before the match started had she been playing a stronger opponent. 'I knew I had a chance against Virginia and thought

That's as bad as it gets. This is one of the most devastating losses I've ever had. I was moving so poorly, my feet felt as if they were size 25s. I'm not going to break every racket in my bag although that would make me feel better.

Jan-Michael Gambill, following the loss of his two-sets-to-one lead over Chris Woodruff.

Above left: Jan-Michael Gambill quenches his thirst before facing another barrage of serves from fellow American, Chris Woodruff (far left), who upset him in the first round.

Left: Virginia Ruano Pascual gave The Championships a dramatic start by beating top-seeded Martina Hingis (above).

capriati v vento • rusedski v pavel • day 1

that once I get past the first round, everything could get better, my mental situation, my feel of the court and everything' she said.

While it was true that she had dropped only seven games in her two previous matches against Ruano Pascual, the Spaniard was obviously match tight and feeling confident after winning both the doubles and the mixed doubles at the French Open. 'It's a dream' she said after receiving a cheering, standing ovation. 'It's frustrating. I tried,' said Hingis. 'Another time I'll have to decide beforehand [when injured] whether it's a good idea to play or not.'

Jennifer Capriati, who had been seeded to meet Hingis in the quarter finals, looked as if she would be the biggest beneficiary of this first-day shock. She looked untroubled as she walked onto Centre Court to continue what John McEnroe had called 'her resurrection' to beat Venezuela's Maria Vento 6-3 6-2. Yet Hingis's earlier departure was also good news for the talented Belgian, eighth-seeded Justine Henin, a runaway 6-1 6-0 winner over Sarah Pitkowski of France, especially as 25th-seeded Chanda Rubin was also removed from her path.

There were no first-round troubles either for fifth-seeded Serena Williams, while three of the most promising Russian prospects, Elena Dementieva, Nadia Petrova and 17-year-old Lina Krasnoroutskaya from Minsk, who has been tipped to be even more successful than the still-injured Anna Kournikova, were also among those making progress although Krasnoroutskaya and tenth-seeded Dementieva, however, both dropped a set, the latter in a 20-point tie-break against the improving American, Allison Bradshaw.

Wimbledon's opening day is traditionally when British players en masse, not just Tim Henman and Greg Rusedski, are in the spotlight and this year, with growing impatience in some quarters about the apparent absence of any challengers for the top two and no one

even among the top 100 in the ladies', that was more true than ever.

Rusedski regularly served in excess of 130 mph but still took more than two-and-a-half hours to overcome the Romanian, Andrei Pavel 7-6 6-7 7-6 6-2. With Pavel also thumping down hefty first serves, tie-breaks were hardly

Jennifer Capriati (left) made a spirited start to her bid for the title.

Below: Greg Rusedski ponders on a first-round job going well on his way to beating the Romanian, Andrei Pavel.

unexpected and in the two which he won, Rusedski conceded only a total of three points. In between, one volleying error was sufficient to give his opponent the second-set tie-break 7-5 but at the end of the third, Pavel needed treatment for a sore back and thereafter Rusedski sailed on.

Henman's 6-1 6-1 6-1 win over Russian qualifier Artem Derepasko on No. 2 Court, was tougher than it looked. At least that was so in the opening set before Henman, whose serve did not always do him favours, became used to the court and began taking the sting out of the cracking returns by the Muscovite, who held serve only twice during the match.

As Henman said 'It always takes time to settle when you're playing someone you know very little about for the first time.' That would not be the case in the second round when the challenge would come from Worthing's Martin Lee, who made good use of his wild card with an impressive 6-4 6-3 6-1 defeat of the experienced veteran Italian, Gianluca Pozzi.

There were two other British winners on the day, Barry Cowan, who could never have dreamed when he beat fellow countryman, Mark Hilton, 6-3 6-2 7-6, what drama awaited him against Sampras in the second round and Karen Cross, who, free from the pressures of having to prove herself after dropping out of tennis full time, beat Holland's Yvette Basting. No joy, though, for four other British wild cards, Louise Latimer, Lucie Ahl, Julie Pullin and Anne Keothavong or for Luke Milligan, who had at least earned his stripes by winning through three rounds at qualifying only to find himself facing eighth-seeded Spaniard, Juan Carlos Ferrero.

Luke Milligan (above) had battled his way through three qualifying rounds for the right to face eighth-seeded Juan Carlos Ferrero on a day when six other British players were trying to justify their wild cards — clockwise, from the top, they were Mark Hilton, Karen Cross, Anne Keothavong, Lucie Ahl, Julie Pullin and Martin Lee.

massu v childs · collin v loit

No first-round joy for former British champions, Lee Childs (below) and Hannah Collin (bottom right), although Holland's Peter Wessels won plenty of admiration for his many winners even though he lost in straight sets to Andre Agassi.

day 2 • vacek v rafter • asagoe v williams, v.

Pat Rafter (opposite) was pleased to come through his first-round match against Daniel Vacek (below) with no recurrence of his arm injury but Tommy Haas (bottom) was one of three players who failed to finish his match on the day. He was suffering from gastric and back problems.

double faulted for the first time in the match — twice! Later, though, having been reassured by fellow Dutch player, Jan Siemerink, who had been watching, he admitted that the call had been correct. Thereafter Agassi stepped up the pressure. He broke in the opening game of the second set with the sweetest of backhand passes and kept Wessels guessing with his impressive variety of serves. It was Agassi's 163rd match win at a Grand Slam, lifting him to sixth equal with Boris Becker on a list headed by Jimmy Connors with 233.

Hewitt, the feisty Australian, who took his winning run to 11 with a 6-1 6-2 6-4 victory over Sweden's Magnus Gustafsson, was eager to dismiss the idea that he should be regarded as a favourite for the title while at the same time he said 'I'm not afraid to step out there against anyone on grass.'

Rafter's biggest relief after his 6-2 7-6 6-3 defeat of the Czech Republic's Daniel Vacek was that there had been no sign of fresh pain in his racket arm — an injury which had once again limited the amount the previous year's runner-up had been able to play.

Next in line for Hewitt would be the strapping 20-year-old Taylor Dent, born and tennis bred in the United States,

whose father Phil, an Australian Davis Cup player, was a Wimbledon doubles finalist in 1977, while his mother, Betty Ann Grubb, was also a successful player of the ladies' tour. Dent was a 6-0 6-1 6-4 winner over twice former French Open champion, Sergi Bruguera of Spain, and, like his father, showed immense power in his all-out serve-and-volley approach.

What a difference a year makes. Vladimir Voltchkov of Belarus, who the previous summer had reached the semi-finals as a qualifier, lost in the first round this time to newcomer Mikhail Youzhny, a tidy, sturdy hitter from Russia.

One extraordinary feature of the day was that three players among the men, Wayne Ferreira, Tommy Haas and Michael Llodra, all failed to finish their matches for a variety of reasons as the first round toll of seeds in this event grew to 11. Ferreira trailed 7-6 6-3 3-0 to the Russian, Andrei Stoliarov, when he was forced to retire with breathing problems following a recent attack of asthma. Haas was suffering from a combination of gastric and back problems when he retired 6-4 5-7 6-1 3-0 against Zimbabwe's Wayne Black and French qualifier Llodra went over on an ankle at 1-2 in the fifth set after clawing back a two-sets deficit against Felix Mantilla.

Although Amelie Mauresmo and Barbara Schett both dropped a set, it was a relatively quiet day in the ladies' singles. Venus Williams made a successful start to the defence of her title, though without looking particularly alert during a patchy 6-2 6-3 win against Shinobu Asagoe of Japan. On the other hand it was the first match the American had played since mid-May. Lindsay Davenport, who had only returned to the game for the first time since March to win in Eastbourne a week earlier, was philosophical about the many unforced errors in her 6-3 6-3 win against Martina Sucha of Slovakia. 'I've learned that all that really matters is getting through the first couple of rounds. My knee is 100 per cent now so I can get better and better.'

Barbara Schett (above) had to recover from a set down to Slovenian qualifier, Maja Matevzic. Venus Williams (right) kept cool and well in control against Japan's Shinobu Asagoe, while Amelie Mauresmo (main picture) also looked confident ahead of the shock awaiting her in the next round.

THE CHAMPIONSHIPS
WIMBLEDON

Three visions of Cowan (below and right), seen acknowledging the ovation he deserved.

By Pete Sampras's own admission, Day Three at Wimbledon could have ended in arguably the biggest upset in the history of The Championship. Although he insisted, when the threat was over, that he never felt in danger of losing his second-round match to Barry Cowan after the Lancashire left-hander had wiped out his two-sets lead with booming serves and flashing forehand service returns, it was 'about as close as it gets.'

Indeed Cowan, a modest 265 on the ATP entry list, was only the fourth player to stretch the remarkable American to a fifth set in Sampras's 13 Wimbledon visits — the others had been Goran Ivanisevic, twice, most recently in the 1998 final, Andre Agassi and Petr Korda. The champion, despite the outward calm he demonstrated, accepted that 'once you go into a fifth set on grass anything can happen' and that as Cowan whittled away a 4-0 deficit in the set, it became 'a dogfight'.

That was certainly the case in the seventh game of that final set when Cowan, with the No. 1 Court crowd roaring their support, twice created the chance to break back to 3-4. Yet as so often over the years, it was then that Sampras's intuitive and extraordinary ability to escape impending disaster at Wimbledon proved his salvation once again. He not only saved the first break point with an ace — but also the second and, considering that he was serving to a left-hander's forehand, that took courage.

As Cowan, who has spent much of his career out of the limelight in Challenger events trying to make enough money to cover his costs, said 'I definitely had him on the ropes. I could see that from his reaction when he hit the ace on that first break point. It's just a shame when I had a little sniff of a chance that he came up with the aces... but that's why he's won seven out of eight Wimbledons. As I walked off court

Previous page: The packed crowd on The Hill is totally caught up in the excitement on No. 1 Court as Barry Cowan brilliantly served his way back from two sets down and went so close to upsetting Pete Sampras, whose anxiety is reflected in the picture below.

The Centre Court here is probably the most prestigious place to play tennis. To get to play here at such a young age is a privilege. I had goosebumps just walking out there. It's kind of majestic.

Andy Roddick, 18, after his second-round defeat of Sweden's Thomas Johansson.

Andy Roddick's fan club is rewarded with his autograph after the 18-year-old American had beaten Thomas Johansson (top), Sweden's most accomplished player on grass courts.

[beaten 6-3 6-2 6-7 4-6 6-3] I felt disappointed but I thought I acquitted myself well and hope this can be the start of better things' he said.

Cowan, a Liverpool soccer supporter, had drawn inspiration from listening to a record of the Kop singing 'You'll Never Walk Alone' during the changeovers. He certainly was not walking alone after he had played a wonderfully inspired third set and held his break in the fourth set to draw level. Despite losing, it had been a noble failure as he joined the 'famous for 15 minutes' club and won the admiration not only of the crowd but his growing army of fans watching the large screen, on The Hill outside.

Yet if Cowan was frustrated by having gone so close to writing himself into tennis history, the sight of Sampras wobbling so badly once he lost his concentration in the third set tie-break, must have given adding encouragement to those waiting in the wings to take on the American in future rounds.

These included Tim Henman, who had taken only two sets off Sampras in three Wimbledon meetings. For once he and Rusedski, who earlier in the day had both moved into the third round, were overshadowed by another British player. Henman, who had politely declined the offer John McEnroe had made to become his coach, won comfortably enough, 6-2 6-3 6-4, against fellow British player, Martin Lee, in a low-key match on Centre Court, in front of a subdued crowd reluctant to show partisan support on either side.

Equally, Rusedski wavered only once in his 6-1 6-3 6-4 defeat of Zimbabwe's Byron Black and then it was when he was serving for the match and had to rescue the sole break point against him. Otherwise the left-hander was in near-faultless form. It was not only the Rusedski serve which worked well, as one had come to expect, including 13 aces, the fastest of them at 135 mph, but also his groundstrokes. It seemed to augur well for his next challenge from Spain's Juan Carlos Ferrero, who had

shown how quickly he was coming to terms with a surface many of his countrymen say is 'only fit for cows' by persisting well for a 7-6 4-6 6-3 6-7 6-3 victory over the Australian, Jason Stoltenberg, a former semi-finalist, making his final Wimbledon appearance.

Later in the day, the Centre Court crowd took their first look at Andy Roddick, the all-action American teenage prodigy and were immediately captivated by his tennis and his personality. The 18-year-old showed stunning maturity in his impressive 7-6 6-1 4-6 7-6 defeat of Sweden's Thomas Johansson. No teenager had made a bigger impact on his first Centre Court appearance since Boris Becker, when he was on his way to becoming the youngest men's singles champion at the age of 17 in 1985. Wonderful pick-ups from inches off the ground and tremendous pace about the court left no one in any doubt that this was only the first of what could be many more appearances for him on the main stage. And Roddick's charming approach continued long afterwards when he won even more hearts by patiently signing dozens of autographs as he left the scene of his victory.

Johansson, the 11th seed and winner of two pre-Wimbledon grass court tournaments, paid a heavy price for unforced errors in both the tie-breaks, especially the second of them when, at 2-1 down, he netted a backhand volley and was then beaten by another of those rasping forehand drive winners down the line from the exuberant teenager, which so often brought gasps of amazement from the crowd.

Meanwhile Goran Ivanisevic, who would be the next to try and contain the young American lion, had followed up his 21 aces in the opening round with 35 more as he played almost perfectly after nervously losing the first set tie-break for a 6-7 6-3 6-4 6-4 win over Spain's 21st-seeded Carlos Moya.

Marat Safin, the third-seeded Russian, still not wholly recovered from his back injury, also advanced — but only

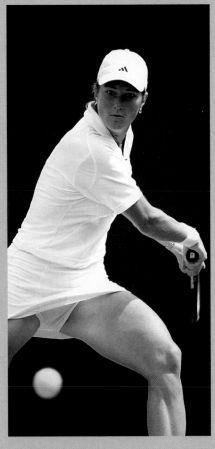

Rusedski (left) in thoughtful mood on his way to beating Byron Black while Justine Henin (below) was often under pressure before resisting Kristie Boogert (below left) in three sets.

Tim Henman (left) had a comfortable Centre-Court win over fellow British player, Martin Lee, on a day when Goran Ivanisevic (above right) won a superb contest of contrasting styles against Carlos Moya and Juan Carlos Ferrero (right) was made to sweat the whole way by Jason Stoltenberg.

safin v nestor • rittner v williams, s. • day 3

after Canadian Daniel Nestor had become the fifth man to retire in the singles. He injured his ankle at one set all and 2-1 down. 'I'm happy he retired. It would have been a very big problem to beat him' said Safin.

It was very much as you would expect among the ladies. The only upset was the premature farewell to Arantxa Sanchez Vicario, the runner-up in 1995 and 1966 when she was beaten 7-6 7-5 in her 15th visit to The Championships by the 21-year-old American, Lilia Osterloh. After losing a first-set tie-break, Sanchez needed treatment for a wrist injury before being broken at 5-5 in the second set but sportingly insisted 'That's not what caused me to lose. I made too many unforced errors.'

Osterloh, who had reached the last 16 in Wimbledon 2000, then had former champion Conchita Martinez, a 7-5 6-4 winner over another American, Sandra Cacic in her sights. The principal ladies' singles focus on the day, though, was on Serena Williams, Jennifer Capriati and Virginia Ruano Pascual, the Spaniard who had knocked out Martina Hingis 48 hours earlier. It proved to have been a short-lived success, for Pascual bowed to Russian teenager, Lina Krasnoroutskaya 6-3 7-6. Williams beat Germany's Barbara Rittner 6-4 6-0 but was then given a sound public scolding by her father, Richard, for having played so poorly. She admitted : 'I wasn't playing well today so I'm gonna practise really hard.'

Capriati was given a huge reception as she walked out and proceeded to reward the crowd with a whole series of pounding groundstrokes which carried her from 4-2 in the first set to 5-0 in the second on the way to a 6-3 6-1 defeat of Francesca Schiavone.

After a first-round defeat the previous year, Justine Henin was hoping at least to emulate her achievement of reaching the French Open semi-finals but the eighth seed had to demonstrate her considerable determination and tenacity to fend off a tremendous challenge by qualifier Kristie Boogert. The

Dutch player looked far more comfortable on the grass for almost two sets but suddenly at a set and 2-5 down, her nerve folded and Henin at last took advantage of one of the break point opportunities she had been missing to achieve a 5-7 7-5 6-2 recovery.

It earned her a third-round match against the American, Lisa Raymond, a quarter finalist the year before, who outclassed the only surviving British girl, Karen Cross, 6-0 6-1, in a mere 40 minutes. It was not exactly what the Exeter girl would have hoped for from her last Wimbledon match.

Only Marat Safin's serve (left) was keeping him in his second-round match against Daniel Nestor when the Canadian had to retire with an injured ankle.

Below: a happy Serena Williams thanks the crowd for their cheers after an easy win over Barbara Rittner.

THE CHAMPIONSHIPS
WIMBLEDON

Inset top left: The Wombles returned to Wimbledon.

Lleyton Hewitt (left) prevailed in a titanic battle against Taylor Dent (above).

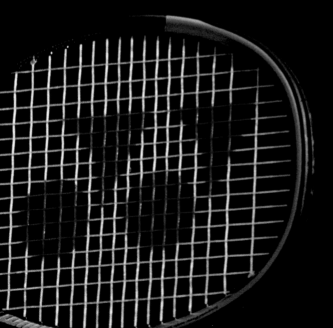

For the second day in succession, Wimbledon's best was kept to last... well almost last, for one marathon match, Cedric Pioline against the Russian, Andrei Stoliarov, was halted with the court becoming slippery close to 9 pm, immediately after the Frenchman had saved two match points to level at 5-5 in the fifth. Pioline eventually lost the final set 12-10 the next day.

The Centre-Court clock had just clicked past 8.30 pm when the contest which had most gripped another all-time record attendance, of 41,440, and forced BBC 2 to delay their normal programme schedule, ended as the crowd rose as one in appreciation of a brilliant battle featuring two 20-year-olds, as bold as they were brave.

Lleyton Hewitt, whose exhilarating style and defiant resistance were already well documented and Taylor Dent, the sturdy American, had treated them to more than three hours of undiluted combat.

In the end Hewitt, who had missed two match points, one of them with a double fault, survived what had been a devastating display of serving and a host of other spectacularly powerful winners by his raw but exciting opponent, to win 1-6 7-5 6-3 6-7 6-3. His happiness, as well as his relief, was evident as the Australian fell back full length on the court and considered how tight it had been.

Dent began like a whirlwind and, despite one or two lulls, gave Hewitt one fright after another. Maybe for the connoisseurs the match was too serve-dominated. Dent won 100 points with his serve, 22 of them aces, and Hewitt 97. On the other hand there were surely enough adventurous, exhilarating and audacious winners from both men in between to satisfy everyone.

The opening game set the tone. Dent, a qualifier, began with two aces, the first at 123 mph, the second at 132 mph and then a service winner at 138 mph. Not long afterwards another serve thundered down at 145 mph although

hewitt v dent • delgado v agassi • day 4

that was called a fault. Then in the fourth-set tie-break, when his reprieve in the previous game had suddenly broadened his shoulders even more, his service winner for a 4-1 lead was 144 mph, the fastest ever timed on the Centre Court. Yet there were also 17 double faults which cost Dent dearly.

Hewitt's obvious hope early on must have been that Dent's storming style would blow itself out. But that did not happen and in the end it was because Hewitt, a supreme counter-puncher, proved himself more consistently effective with his returns that he took his unbeaten record on grass for the year to 14.

Naturally as Barry Cowan remained the focus of attention for many media outlets on the day after his heroic near-miss against Pete Sampras the night before, there were hopes that Jamie Delgado and Arvind Parmar, the two remaining wild-carded British players still alive, might produce some giant-killing threats of their own.

It was asking a lot. Delgado, who strokes stylish winners round the court well enough but lacks a truly killer shot at this level, was playing former champion, Andre Agassi. The 6ft 4in Parmar, whose reluctance to come in and volley behind a serve, which so often provides

Andre Agassi (opposite) was too agile, powerful and experienced for Britain's Jamie Delgado (below).

the opportunity for him to do so, was again all too evident, was taking on seventh-seeded Yevgeny Kafelnikov.

For a while, Parmar, who delayed his first approach to the net until the opening point of the tenth game, took advantage of some nervy play by the Russian former winner of French Open and Australian Open titles and won the first set. Kafelnikov's uncertainty had been exacerbated by an early rain break but British optimism was not sustained for long on Court 2. Once Kafelnikov, who was coming in behind every serve and increasingly scoring with first volleys, settled down, there was only ever going to be one outcome.

Perhaps had Parmar, who could be forgiven for being mentally tired after his marathon five-setter in the first round, taken one of the three break points he had for a 2-1 lead in the third set, it might have been different but his spirits, as well as his body seemed to flag as Kafelnikov ran through nine of the last ten games for a 6-7 6-3 6-3 6-1 win.

The day got better and better, at least in theory, for Kafelnikov. As he waited to discover whether he would face either the Argentinian, George Canas or the Dane, Kenneth Carlsen in the third round, he said 'Obviously I want to avoid Carlsen because lefties always bring troubles, especially on this surface.' Canas obliged, winning a marathon after two rain breaks 7-5 4-6 6-7 7-6 6-4 — though as we were to discover two days later, it was not such a good outcome for Kafelnikov after all.

Delgado started well against Agassi but it soon became obvious that he would not be able to sustain rallies often enough if he was to pose a credible threat to the 1992 champion and was beaten 6-2 6-4 6-3. 'In the second set maybe I felt like I was getting into it with a couple of half chances but against somebody as good as he is, half chances have to be taken — and I couldn't, but it was a good experience to play someone like him. I enjoyed it a lot' Delgado said.

Above: Delgado's enthusiastic supporters.

There was initial concern that Pat Rafter's injured elbow might be playng up again when he played so lethargically for most of the two sets against Slava Dosedel. Instead, as the Australian confessed after his 7-5 4-6 6-4 6-1 win: 'Slava is a very unpredictable player and it took me some time to work out his game.'

The 14 seeds on duty as the second-round matches in the ladies' singles were being completed, all recorded the victories expected of them, with both the second and third seeds, Venus Williams and Lindsay Davenport leading the way. Williams, though still not consistently enough at her best, galloped to a 6-3 6-2 win over Daniela Hantuchova, a Slovakian making her Wimbledon debut while 25-year-old former champion, Lindsay Davenport, won convincingly enough, 6-4 6-2 against the Australian, Alicia Molik, and then revealed that she was already contemplating retirement.

'I started playing when I was 16 and being on the tour is a very difficult lifestyle' said the American. 'It's especially so for the girls because they start a lot earlier than the guys and often get success much earlier but I didn't have my family travelling with me and there are definitely times when you get bored and lonely.'

She said she was 'looking for three more years and then I'd like to do other things, such as have kids at a young enough age so that I can enjoy them. I think it was one of the coolest things when Steffi [Graf] left the game just when she felt she wanted to.'

Amelie Mauresmo, Jelena Dokic and Kim Clijsters, all of whom had been mentioned before the tournament to at least make waves if not win the title, were also straight-set winners on the day with Dokic, a much more elegant mover than when she beat Martina Hingis in the first round two years earlier, using her aggressive range of shots well as she beat the American, Jennifer Hopkins, 6-2 6-4.

kafelnikov v parmar • dosedel v rafter

Above: Yevgeny Kafelnikov (above) lost the first set to Arvind Parmar but went on to keep the British player at full stretch.

Venus Williams (opposite) was always in command against Daniela Hantuchova (bottom right) of the Slovak Republic.

Left: Total focus and determination by Jelena Dokic.

Below left: Alicia Molik's serve tested Lindsay Davenport well in the first set.

THE CHAMPIONSHIPS
WIMBLEDON

roddick v ivanisevic • day 5

Patriotism and sentiment dominated Day Five. After an hour's initial delay to the Centre and No. 1 Court programmes because of drizzle, Greg Rusedski produced arguably his most impressive tennis at The Championships to overcome Juan Carlos Ferrero, a Spanish novice on grass, though eager now to learn and improve. Late in the evening, after a tense set and a half, Tim Henman secured his place in the second week for a commendable sixth year in succession by recovering to repeat his French Open victory over Holland's Sjeng Schalken.

What happened in between these encouraging results for British tennis, however, earned just as many cheers and even a few happy tears as Goran Ivanisevic at last produced a silver-lining result to his *annus horribilis* by taming the year's most exciting teenager, Andy Roddick.

Ivanisevic has always insisted that there is more than just one Goran on court when he is playing. There is 'Goran the wild' and 'Goran the gifted'. Too often in the past two years when a chronic shoulder had reduced one of the game's greatest entertainers to a morose wreck, the former held sway. And for a few worrying moments when, even at this stage of the tournament, he rushed into missing two match points against Roddick, who was equally downcast after double faulting to put the Croatian in control, it looked as if 'Goran the wild' might once again snatch a defeat from the jaws of victory.

It was then that Ivanisevic called up what he called No. 3 Goran, 'the emergency guy', the one who can come on and say 'calm down'. He's the brain man. At that stage the other two Gorans were both nervous. One was rushing; the other was rushing even more. Then the third came and said 'Guys, relax. It's a lovely court. Just calm down.'

Previous page: It's party time, with a barbecue, for these overnight campers in the queue.

Opposite: Goran Ivanisevic recovers from a set down to outlast Andy Roddick (below) in a gritty serving battle on No. 1 Court.

day 5 • rusedski v ferrero

Above: Juan Carlos Ferrero found Greg Rusedski (opposite) at the top of his form, in their third-round clash.

Grand Slam which I don't think anyone would have bet on before I came here. Just perfect.'

Ivanisevic, a wild card, paid tribute to Roddick — 'a great player already whose going to be even better' — but also pinpointed the youngster's moments of immaturity such as the reckless drop shot at 5-4 in the tie-break which probably cost him the first set.

This, though, was a match ruthlessly controlled by the Ivanisevic serve, which achieved a 72 per cent first-serve success rate. Rallies were few. There were only two of the left-hander's service games in which he did not serve at least one ace. The 43 games were completed at an average rate of just over 2.5 minutes.

As Roddick said 'It's tough when you feel as if you don't even have a chance in return games. You feel pretty helpless. It's not fun. You see it on TV when he's acing guys but now I was the guy getting aced. At the end I told him "That was impressive, I'm cheering for you the rest of the way." '

By the time Ivanisevic came off court he already knew that his next challenger would be Rusedski, whom he had beaten in all eight of their previous encounters. Yet just as the three-times former runner-up had completed his first week of The Championships with his best performance for many moons, so too had the British left-hander as he crushed Ferrero 6-1 6-4 6-4. Although it was only Ferrero's fourth match on grass, there had been indications in his previous match against Jason Stoltenberg, that he was starting to feel more comfortable on the surface.

Rusedski put paid to that. Especially in the opening set, when the only blemish was the way Rusedski lost his own serve with some slapdash volleys, the home favourite served splendidly, returned potently and generally hit his groundstrokes with a consistent length and penetration which simply denied his opponent the chance to get going.

'It was the kind of performance I needed to get off court quick so that I

Moments later Ivanisevic boomed down two more aces, taking his total for the day to 41, just five short of his own one-match Wimbledon record and 98 in three matches for the week. The still-lean left-hander was ecstatic. Off came his shirt as he bared his chest and thumped on his heart in response to the standing ovation from an equally happy crowd. 'I just don't know what to say. I'm through to the second week of a

day 5 • schalken v henman

could save my energy for next week' Rusedski said. He broke, with the help of a Ferrero double fault for 3-2 in the second set and the same scenario helped him break again for 2-1 in the third. Ferrero had one chance to break back but Rusedski firmly prevented that with another fine kicking serve supported by a high forehand volley before serving out to love.

Henman, who been dominant almost throughout their match in Paris a month earlier, started indifferently against 26th-seeded Schalken, a specialist in five-set marathons at Wimbledon in previous years, especially in year 2000 when he ultimately lost 20-18 in the fifth after a 5 hours 5 minutes match — a record for one match contained within a single day — against Mark Philippoussis.

There was an early shock for Henman. Schalken, tall, lean and angular, broke him in the first game and again in the 11th and although Henman saved three set points and also had a break point, his backhand flew wide as he attempted to return another big serve on the fourth set point.

Yet as the second set unfolded, it soon became clear that Henman was stepping up the pace and — just as importantly — cutting down on the errors. Once Schalken double faulted to give him a break to lead 4-2, the whole tone of the match was different. The third set was the key. In the extraordinary third and fourth games, first Schalken held from 0-40 and then Henman did precisely the same one game later. Then on a second break point at 4-4, Henman struck a glorious forehand winning pass which seemed to unsettle the Dutchman for he double faulted twice in three consecutive service games in the fourth set and was beaten 5-7 6-3 6-4 6-2.

Although Henman had not played his most authoritative tennis, as he said 'I had some real pressure to deal with and I'm coming back on Monday, That's the most important thing.' Also coming back would be Pete Sampras, Marat Safin, Todd Martin and another

excitingly gifted newcomer to such heights, Roger Federer.

Before this year Federer had never won a match on two previous visits to Wimbledon but thanks in no small measure to the 13 break points he had saved against Belgium's Xavier Malisse in the second round here he was, the centre of attention. For after his 7-6 6-3 7-6 win over Sweden's Jonas Bjorkman, Sampras was next on his list.

'To meet Pete on the Centre Court at Wimbledon is like a dream come true. He was one of my idols when I was a kid and to play him here is just great' said the 19-year-old Swiss right hander, who had underlined his growing mental strength by winning the first tie-break against Bjorkman 7-4 and the second, in the third set, 7-2.

Sampras, meanwhile, had progressed easily, though without much conviction on his returns, with a 6-4 6-4 7-5 win over Sargis Sargsian of Armenia. The brightest moment of a routine contest on No. 1 Court came when Sampras slipped as he went to make a return in the second set and he finished up sitting on the grass with the ball inside the leg of his shorts. He teased the ball boy who had run over to retrieve the ball but then realised it was nowhere to be seen, by pointing out to him where it could be found and indicating that he could take it if he wished. Politely, just as you would expect from any well trained Wimbledon ball boy, he declined.

Martin dropped a set in beating Magnus Larsson while Safin struggled to overcome Germany's David Prinosil 7-6 6-3 5-7 1-6 6-3 and then revealed how much his coach, Mats Wilander, had to do to convince the big-serving Russian that he has the game to do well at Wimbledon, by insisting 'grass is not my surface.'

For a fourth day in succession, the ladies' matches tended to be overshadowed by the men although Anke Huber gave the Germans something to enjoy by upsetting 10th-seeded Elena Dementieva 6-0 6-2. Lina Krasnoroutskaya, a 6-3 6-4

Right: Tim Henman defiantly stepped up the pace after dropping the first set to Sjeng Schalken (above) much to the delight of his fans.

raymond v henin • capriati v panova • day 5

winner over Austria's Barbara Schwartz, at least made sure there would be one Russian still alive in the second week.

As for the principal title contenders in the top half of the draw, Jennifer Capriati, Serena Williams and Justine Henin all won in straight sets, though Henin again had to dig deep and find reserves of stamina and defiant spirit to stave off Lisa Raymond 6-4 7-6.

On paper the 6-4 6-4 victory for Capriati over the Russian, Tatiana Panova, seemed straightforward enough. In truth it was a worryingly patchy display by the fourth seed, full of unforced errors. Indeed she trailed 0-2 in the first set, where she also double faulted three times to go 3-4 down — and Panova, using the court and her wide range of shots as impressively as she was fast covering ground, also led 4-1 in the second.

Capriati, who was fortunate that Panova's lack of experience manifested itself in too many indiscreet groundshots just when she looked poised to force a final set, admitted she had been 'lethargic' but blamed it on the frustration of waiting around for the rain to clear and the cold, windy conditions. Everyone was too discreet to remind her that it was the same for her opponent.

Similarly Williams was flattered by the scale of her 6-1 6-2 defeat of the spindly Emanuelle Gagliardi and she knew it. 'I don't think I played at all well today' she said. 'I couldn't get my feet moving and I made a lot of errors' she admitted honestly. She looked much sharper when she and sister Venus returned to court later to beat the French pair, Nathalie Dechy and Amelie Mauresmo 6-3 6-3 in the second round of the ladies' doubles.

Far left: Jennifer Capriati had to fight all the way in the third round to subdue the fast-improving Russian, Tatiana Panova (bottom left), on a day when a mixture of style and dogged determination brought wins also for Sandrine Testud (left) and another gifted young Russian, Lina Krasnoroutskaya (below).

THE CHAMPIONSHIPS WIMBLEDON

SATURDAY 30 JUNE
day6

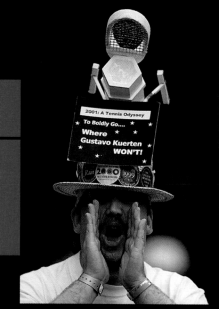

2001: A Tennis Odyssey

To Boldly Go....
Where
Gustavo Kuerten
WON'T!

The sun shone as brightly as the tennis as Lleyton Hewitt (left) withstood a blistering start by Younes El Aynaoui (bottom far left) and Pat Rafter (below) took enough of the key points against the equally charismatic Hicham Arazi (serving far left) to achieve two Australian victories over Morocco.

Australia 2 Morocco 0. That was the other Centre-Court score at the end of Day Six after Pat Rafter and Lleyton Hewitt, the third and fifth seeds, had ended an impressive first week for Hicham Arazi and Younes El Aynaoui, the two most successful players to emerge from their country.

Neither departed without leaving their mark in a way which certainly found favour with the crowd. The tennis before Rafter completed his 7-6 6-4 7-5 victory over Arazi, the impish master of touch and angles, made it a blissful way for the spectators to enjoy a sunny summer evening.

The late Sir Alf Ramsey, who guided England to triumph in soccer's 1966 World Cup once observed in a memorable television interview 'You can't write off the Moroccan or whatever they're called.' Arazi and El Aynaoui, especially the latter, demonstrated that the comment was just as true today.

Rafter had to hold on grimly during the first set when Arazi was freewheeling his way from one exuberant point to the next but at least the Australian's serve was a constant ally, which eventually helped the rest of his serve-and-volley game to fall into place.

Earlier on a day when the Australians were feeling bruised — though certainly not humble — after the thrashing of the Wallabies in the first Rugby Union test against the British Lions, Hewitt had been pushed all the way in a contest full of hard-hitting rallies before overcoming El Aynaoui 7-5 5-7 6-4 7-6.

Hewitt's approach was as predictable as El Aynaoui's was subtle and varied, though both were reluctant to venture more than occasionally beyond the service court. It was the youngster who tended to make a bigger impact on more of the biggest points, especially in the fourth-set tie-break. Both deserved the

rapturous reception they were given at the end.

The only major seeding upset of the day in the bottom half of the draw came on Court 2 when Yevgeny Kafelnikov, the seventh seed, again pressed the self-destruct button and plunged to defeat against Guillermo Canas, a conventional clay-court player, who had only once before seriously attracted notice in Britain when he beat Tim Henman in Paris.

Kafelnikov, who won the first set comfortably enough but went walkabout in the second, led 3-0 in the third before conceding six consecutive games in an all too typically rash, careless fashion and then, most disastrously of all, double faulted three times in a row when serving for the fourth at 5-3. Kafelnikov who meekly surrendered the fourth-set tie-break was asked 'How did you come to lose that match?' 'Good question, I wish I knew' he replied after Canas became the first Argentine since Jose Luis Clerc 22 years earlier to reach the last 16.

The day had begun with three Russians on duty but with the unseeded Andrei Stoliarov going down to the more experienced German, Nicolas Kiefer, only Mikhail Youzhny, a Wimbledon

newcomer, survived to join fourth-seeded Marat Safin who had already reached the fourth round in the top half of the draw. And Youzhny did so when 20th-seeded Frenchman, Fabrice Santoro suffered a shoulder injury which forced him to quit when two sets and a break down.

It was very much plain sailing for second-seeded Andre Agassi on No. 1 Court. He took less than an hour and a half to dismiss Chile's Nicolas Massu 6-3 6-1 6-1 in a match which will probably only be remembered for the way he and a ball girl accidentally collided during the changeover after the first game of the second set.

Agassi stayed on course to become the first player to win the men's singles title in his 30s since Arthur Ashe in 1975 by remaining on the baseline for most of the match honing his ground-strokes. Just occasionally he stepped up the pace to underline his supremacy. For the most part he was content just to test his opponent's stamina by forcing him to chase back and forth until the point was over. Only once did Agassi go in behind his serve and that was only to save the sole break point against him at 5-1 in the second set after 53 minutes.

Meanwhile, 24th-seeded Nicolas

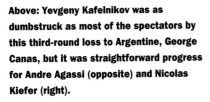

Above: Yevgeny Kafelnikov was as dumbstruck as most of the spectators by this third-round loss to Argentine, George Canas, but it was straightforward progress for Andre Agassi (opposite) and Nicolas Kiefer (right).

sampras v federer • day 7

It was bound to happen some time and the possibility had never looked so strong as it did this year. Even so it was still almost hard to believe, when, at 6.20 pm exactly on Day Seven, the King finally lost his crown on the Centre Court. After 31 consecutive Wimbledon victories and a stunning seven titles in eight years, Pete Sampras was spectacularly deposed by Switzerland's Roger Federer, the only teenager left in the draw.

Federer, whose talent has been developing apace since he won the junior boy's title three years ago, struggled to choke back the tears after delivering a winning forehand service return down the line on his first match point against the champion who has been his lifelong idol.

His was a triumph which naturally brought unimaginable joy to a brilliantly gifted new contender and also closed an amazing chapter in the history of men's tennis in general, not just at The Championships. With the game's greatest grass court player no longer barring the way, the fight for the succession seemed sure to intensify, with former champion, Andre Agassi and the previous year's runner-up, Pat Rafter, regarded as leaders of the pack.

There had been doubts all along both inside and outside the locker room about Sampras's ability to equal Bjorn Borg's achievement of winning the title five years in succession. The customary zest and authority has been missing for some time and his last title had been at Wimbledon 12 months earlier.

Yet if there was to be some salvation for him this year, one felt it might still be at the All England Club, where his inspiration and instinct for survival have never been greater — demonstrated again in the second round against Lancastrian Barry Cowan.

Federer, though, a 19-year-old dollar millionaire, living at home with his parents and sister in Basle, where he first learned the game at the age of three on court with his South African mother, Lynette, proved himself a rather special challenger.

Just like Sampras had done so often, Federer, who at the age of 12 had been forced to choose between a soccer or tennis career, played much of his best tennis when the pressure was at its greatest. That was especially so when the top seed had two chances for a break at 4-4 in the final set which would have allowed them to serve out for what would have been his 100th grass-court victory.

Yet instead of converting the sort of pass which in previous years would have been routine, Sampras drove the ball directly towards an opponent who boldly stood his ground and volleyed away a telling winner. On his second opportunity, Sampras's forehand into the net was a tired, almost forlorn effort which suggested that this time the noose really was tightening.

Federer's stinging service return on the first point of the 11th game added to the pressure. The volley errors which followed merely confirmed the ending of a reign. Federer, who saved a point for the opening set at 5-6 in a 9-7 tie-break when Sampras netted a forehand return off what he complained was a faulty serve, could have won in straight sets.

He had six break points, spread over two separate games in the second set which he lost 7-5 when, having clawed back from 0-40 to deuce, he made a hash of a high forehand volley on the fourth set point. That blunder, though, was nothing compared to one which effectively cost Sampras the third set. On break point at 4-4, Sampras soared with apparent confidence to put away one of his rousing slam dunk smashes but overhit by a mile. Embarrassed as well as annoyed, he hid his face in his hands.

As the excitement mounted so Sampras's serve at last began to give him fresh hope but Federer's resistance remained formidable. He saved two break points in the eighth game with winning serves, while from 0-30 two games later, there were two aces, a service winner and a third ace. It reflected extraordinary composure and maturity, as well as skill by a superb prospect who by then had

Previous page: The end of an era. Pete Sampras fights back the tears as he congratulates Roger Federer on becoming the first player in 32 matches to beat him at The Championships. The 19-year-old Swiss played brilliantly and, left, deservedly took the applause from the crowd.

Opposite, top: Greg Rusedski's serve crucially let him down at key times against Goran Ivanisevic but Marat Safin (bottom left) played the grass-court match of his life to beat Arnaud Clement.

Far right: Photographers from round the world capture the drama and excitement.

won 43 matches on the tour during the year, second only to Lleyton Hewitt, and the nine break points he saved against Sampras followed 33 in his three previous matches.

When Sampras brilliantly served his way through a 7-2 fourth-set tie-break after a netted backhand volley by Federer, the odds were still on the champion, especially as he had won all of his five previous Wimbledon matches which had gone to five sets. Federer, though, simply would not yield. He matched

Sampras ace for ace, 25-25, forehand for forehand until suddenly it was the American who faltered.

Federer, seeded (15) at a Grand Slam for a first time, fell on the ground in disbelief as well as joy. He was the first player since Richard Krajicek in the 1996 quarter finals to have beaten Sampras at The Championships.

The typically dignified and gracious beaten champion said 'Obviously I'm very disappointed but he played great. I lost to a really really good player today — a great shot-maker who won the big points. It just wasn't to be. I came up a little bit short. I knew my run wasn't going to last forever. Over the years I've often been a bit fortunate.' As for the future? 'There's no need to panic and think I can't come back and win here again. I always feel I can win here.'

Meanwhile Federer, now in with a chance of becoming the first teenage champion since Boris Becker won for a second time in 1986, was all smiles as he celebrated 'the biggest win in my life. It feels unbelievable. I'm so happy with my performance' he said. 'I fought from the first point to the last. Obviously it's something special for me.'

It was also a rather special day for Marat Safin and Goran Ivanisevic. Safin, despite his misgivings about playing on grass, was in quite devastating, attacking form as he swept aside Frenchman, Arnaud Clement 6-0 6-3 6-2, regularly marching to the chair hardly able to contain his pleasure, in stark contrast to the slow frustrated amble so evident while he was trying to find a range and rhythm in earlier rounds.

The crowd's happiness at watching Ivanisevic sustain what no one had thought possible was diminished somewhat because it was at the expense of Britain's unseeded Greg Rusedski. The atmosphere at the start was tremendous, just as it was when Rusedski fought back from 0-5 to 5-6 in the first-set tie-break. Overall, though, it was a disappointingly modest display by him. Not once did Rusedski reach break point against the

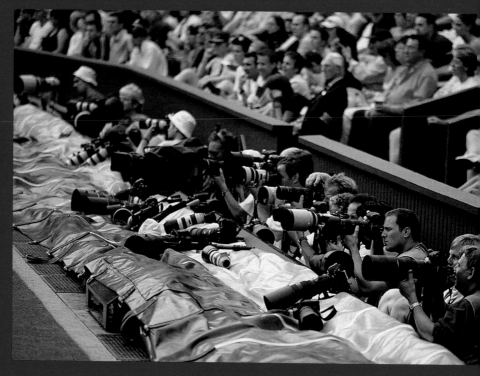

Ivanisevic serve and he was none too effective either with his own serve as what had promised to be a heavyweight contest ultimately became a mis-match. Ivanisevic won 7-6 6-4 6-4.

There were, though, other gripping men's matches wherever one looked with Mikhail Youzhny like a jack-in-the-box reaching and returning drop shots quite spectacularly as he took the first set from Pat Rafter before the Australia's serve-and-volley game began to slot into place and he impressively turned things round to win 2-6 6-3 6-2 7-5.

For Rafter's fellow countryman, Lleyton Hewitt, however, it was the end of what had always been a sometimes risky ride. He was beaten after three and a half hours by an inspired Nicolas Escude 4-6 6-4 6-3 4-6 6-4, thereby breaking his sequence of 15 consecutive grass-court victories, which had including taking the Stella Artois and Rosmalen titles.

Hewitt's defeat denied the tournament of a quarter final between Hewitt and Andre Agassi who always looked superior in his 6-3 7-5 7-5 defeat of Germany's Nicolas Kiefer. Escude nevertheless deserved his last eight place, as did Sweden's Thomas Enqvist, who served too consistently as he beat George Canas of Argentina, perhaps the most surprised player to have reached the fourth round, 6-3 6-3 6-1.

As for Tim Henman, he had to wait until well into the early evening before Sampras and Federer had left the Centre Court clear for him, to begin seeking revenge against Todd Martin, the veteran American who had beaten him on the same stage in the quarter finals five years earlier. The early omens were not good for the British number one. A back muscle spasm meant he was moving stiffly for much of the first two sets and Martin, who had taken the first in a tie-break might have won them both for Henman had to save two set points at 5-6, the first with an ace, before he served out with another ace.

That second tie-break could not have been tighter. Martin missed two easy volleys but Henman persisted to win it 7-5. Many of the rallies were long and the minutes were ticking away. With Martin leading 5-4 and about to serve for the third set in rapidly fading light, the players were told that it would be the last game for the day. Martin served out confidently so, at 8.58 pm, Henman went home to ponder over whether his back and his game would enable him to win the remaining two sets the next day.

No disrespect to the ladies, but most of their fourth-round matches were completed so rapidly, with only one of the eight going to three sets, that they were largely neglected on the day. The contest which attracted the most excitement was the first encounter on Centre Court when Jelena Dokic quickly established a 4-2 lead over Lindsay Davenport. Yet, despite threatening other problems for her opponent, she could not quite prevent the American from breaking back immediately and thereafter producing either the winning serve or the powerful forehand necessary to win 7-5 6-4 in 75 minutes.

Serena Williams who, without being at her best, had conceded only eight matches against three previous opponents, brushed aside the more experienced 12th seed Magdalena Maleeva almost contemptuously 6-2 6-1, while Jennifer Capriati took only 58 minutes for her crushing 6-1 6-2 victory over the French player, Sandrine Testud. Had Serena then ventured to No. 2 Court she would have seen big sister, Venus, crush the Russian Nadia Petrova 6-2 6-0 in seven minutes less than that.

A victorious salute (right) from Pat Rafter and typical determination from Andre Agassi, as the quarter finals began to take shape but Lleyton Hewitt's fighting instincts (top right) were not enough against an inspired Nicolas Escude.

Tim Henman (bottom right) was left in suspense overnight when fading light brought a halt to his fourth-round clash with Todd Martin (below right).

Below: Another scorching backhand from Serena Williams as she outclassed Magdalena Maleeva.

rafter v youzhny • henman v martin • day 7

	Miss J. HOPKINS
	Miss E. BALTACHA
	Miss N. DECHY
	Miss M. MATEVZIC
	Miss B. SCHETT
	Miss P. SCHNYDER
	Miss J. NEJEDLY
	Miss J. KANDARR
	Miss A. MEDINA GARRIGUES
	Miss A. MOLIK
	Miss C. CASTANO
	Miss M. SUCHA
	Miss L.A. DAVENPORT
	Miss A. MAURESMO
	Miss N.J. PRATT
	Miss E. DANIILIDOU
	Miss L. BACHEVA
	Miss L. CERVANOVA
	Miss D. BUTH
	Miss C. BLACK
	Miss T. TANASUGARN
	Miss H. NAGYOVA
	Miss A. SERRA-ZANETTI

It may have been ladies' quarter-final day, with another of those always fascinating contests between Jennifer Capriati and Serena Williams topping the bill but it was the unfinished drama from the night before which promised and delivered the most excitement.

Tim Henman knew a bold, brisk start was essential if he was to wipe out the two-sets-to-one deficit hanging over him when bad light had prevented completion of his fourth-round match with Todd Martin. The first of what were to be many huge roars exploded when he gave not only the equally tense crowd within the Centre Court but also the thousands watching on the big screen outside the best possible hint of his attacking intentions with an ace on the first point.

Henman, who has sometimes been guilty in the past of pressing too much when a more cautious approach might have been helpful but just as often not being aggressive enough once the point has started on grass, quickly showed that on this occasion he had the balance

exactly right. Not only that but an early immaculate smash eased fears that the back restrictions, which had twice forced Henman to have treatment on court the night before, was likely to recur.

Instead the physical problems during the match were all with Martin who, increasingly after he had been broken by three great service returns from Henman in the sixth game of the fourth set, was clearly being hampered by his damaged and heavily protected left knee. Although he saved two set points at 2-5, which would have given Henman a greater incentive because he would then have been serving first in the final set, one felt that Martin's resolve was weakening.

Henman must have known that July 3 was the day his Wimbledon involvement had come to an end in four previous years for almost every newspaper, radio and television station had mentioned it that morning but this was an occasion when he was determined that nothing and no one would hold him back. Only once, when he had to save

When I first came here and watched as a five-year-old, I saw the kind of atmosphere there was when Roger beat Pete last night. I've always wanted to be part of that. The Centre Court is as good as it gets. Last night I was struggling with my game, struggling a little with my mind, but today I felt I had to make my presence felt, my intentions clear.

Tim Henman after beating Todd Martin to reach the quarter finals.

Below: Tim Henman accepts congratulations from Todd Martin.

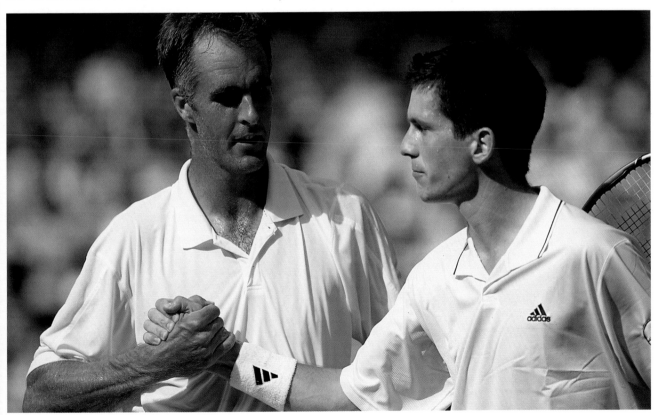

Far left: Quarter-final drama as Serena Williams needed to take a bathroom break before returning to hit more winners against Jennifer Capriati, who needed treatment for a leg injury.

Capriati (above) had the last word, though, as referee Alan Mills kept a close eye on things, and she was ecstatic at the end, (far left) as she waved to her fans.

two break points at 1-2 in the final set was Martin offered a chance to take command. Instead Henman fought his way out of trouble and as so often happens in such circumstances, then broke through himself in the very next game.

Martin's double fault immediately put pressure on the American and Henman, seizing his opportunity, hit two more winning service returns to reach 15-40 before a disheartened backhand by his now limping opponent. It was the beginning of the end.

As Sue Mott wrote in *The Daily Telegraph* 'All we needed were ropes, bell and bucket (especially the bucket) and this [Serena Williams v. Jennifer Capriati] would have been the women's heavyweight championship of the world. Not in terms of poundage but indomitable slugging. Every shot was a punch traded, every lost point a blacked eye. This was brutal. The trainers came on. The girls went off for injury and sick breaks. It was an open-air episode of E.R.'

Williams, who had broken Capriati in her opening service game but immediately sacrificed the initiative with three unforced errors one game later, revealed after her 6-7 7-5 6-3 defeat that she had been suffering from a gastric complaint for four days and that she had been vomiting when she had to make a quick exit from the court at 0-4 in the final set.

The explanation attracted more attention than the tennis, which was a pity because between the mistakes there were many memorable winners from both players. Michelle Gebrian, a trainer with the Women's Tennis Association confirmed that Williams had been seeing a doctor since the weekend but said that no one from the Williams family had told her that Serena had thought of withdrawing even before the third round.

Capriati, who had lost the first tie-break 7-4 after 51 ferocious minutes and then been two points from defeat at 3-5 in the second set, was not impressed or convinced. 'Every time I play her I am pretty much used to something going on

enin • tauziat v williams, v.

there' she said. 'I don't know whether she does it on purpose.'

And later, Lindsay Davenport, who had cut down an overawed Kim Clijsters 6-1 6-2 in 48 minutes, also on Centre Court, added her thoughts.

'It seems like Serena likes to do that against Jennifer. I don't know if it is the losing or if she has some mental thing with Jennifer. A lot of time when she's down something happens with the trainer on court. It happened to me at the U.S. Open when I was beating her. It looks like she doesn't want to take a loss.'

Capriati said she only knew that Williams was sick when her opponent fled and the umpire told her it was 'an emergency'. When she returned Williams also lost the next game — her ninth in succession — but won the next two before overhitting a forehand on the first match point in the ninth game and running off court again. It was not long before she and Venus announced their withdrawal from the doubles, giving Martina Navratilova and Arantxa Sanchez Vicario a walkover into the last eight.

There had been no comparable drama as Venus Williams beat Nathalie Tauziat 7-5 6-1 but the match would still be remembered if only for the way the American went walkabout in such worrying, amazing fashion for 20 minutes in the first set. Having raced to a set point at 5-1 in a mere 18 minutes, it took her another 29 minutes and seven more set points before she won it. 'I think I got a little over-confident and then when she started to play better I felt rushed' said Williams. 'I told myself "You'd better calm down." '

At least she succeeded in that but there was a salutary lesson for the future if she was to retain her title. Williams insisted it would be a one-off loss. It needed to be for even allowing for the way Tauziat, 33, snapped up to make her last Wimbledon singles appearance a real match, the way in which the second seed squandered some of those set points was far from reassuring.

Seven years earlier Conchita Martinez had brought Martina Navratilova's wonderful singles career to an end with a virtuoso display of backhand passes in the final to deny the American a 10th title. This time, in the quarter finals, she was facing Justine Henin, the 19-year-old whose own backhand had been making headlines. Yet the hoped-for fascinating contest between youth and experience never materialised.

Martinez endured what she called 'one of the worst days of my tennis life' in losing 6-1 6-0. Henin, delighted that her forehand was starting to become as much a weapon as the backhand, kept up the pressure well but with the Spaniard's serve embarrassingly weak and her play from the back of the court equally brittle, she had very little to beat.

Elsewhere Max Mirny and Vladimir Voltchkov continued their progress in the men's doubles with a four-sets win over Marc Rosset and Marat Safin, while the unheralded Lancashire junior, Ken Skupski, no longer in an LTA squad, sprang a surprise by maintaining British interest into the last 16 of the boys' singles. The only British player to get into the event through the qualifying competition and the only survivor from ten who started, he hit 15 aces as he beat Sweden's ninth-seeded Robin Soderling 6-4 6-7 6-3. Ross Hutchins, son of former British Davis Cup player, Paul, almost joined him in the third round but was beaten 6-4 4-6 10-8 by Italy's Alberto Brizzi after 2 hours 10 minutes. He had shown great spirit in recovering from 0-3 in the final set and saved three match points before losing on his ninth double fault.

Meanwhile in the girls' singles, the two seeded British players, Elena Baltacha and Anne Keothavong both carried the Union Jack into the last 16. The powerful Baltacha, whose fastest serve was surpassed only by the Williams sisters on the women's leader board during the fortnight, took an hour to beat Dominika Nociarova of Slovakia. Keothavong brushed aside Italy's Lisa Tognetti 6-2 6-0 in 45 minutes.

No joy this time for former champion, Conchita Martinez (top left) or Nathalie Tauziat (top right) who was overpowered by defending champion Venus Williams (below).

Bottom left: Experience, though, was the key as 1999 champion Lindsay Davenport rapidly crushed Kim Clijsters on Centre Court.

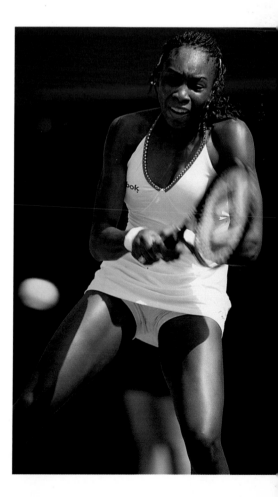

day 9

My matches should carry a health warning.

Tim Henman after another heart-stopping victory over Roger Federer lasting 3 hours 12 minutes.

Left: Tim Henman decisively kept his nerve in a titanic quarter final against Roger Federer (above) who needed treatment from trainer Bill Norris for a groin strain.

The line-up on Day Nine was a connoisseur's dream. It was a glorious combination of players who had already been there and beyond more than once in their careers such as former champion, Andre Agassi, and the 2000 runner-up, Pat Rafter; newcomers to such Wimbledon heights, Marat Safin, Roger Federer, Thomas Enqvist and Nicolas Escude, plus the man revelling in being the wildest of wild cards, Goran Ivanisevic.

Yet for the lucky ones with tickets for Centre Court and the cheering, flag-waving 5,000 who packed the picnic bank in front of the giant screen showing the action, all the focus was on one man, Britain's Tim Henman — and how magnificently he rose to the challenge.

In a dramatic tie-break finish to what proved to be the decisive fourth set, Henman, who admitted he had been 'as tight as a drum,' showed nerves of steel as he reached the Wimbledon semi-finals for a magnificent third time in four years.

The crowd, many even more anxious than him as what looked to be a match-winning lead was whittled away, rose almost as one to celebrate his thrilling 7-5 7-6 2-6 7-6 triumph over Federer. The Swiss 19-year-old who, 48 hours earlier, had brought Pete Sampras's domination of The Championships to an end, had plenty of his own chances and should have won both the tie-breaks but found this an even more mentally challenging experience and in the end it was Henman's success in winning more of the biggest points which gave him the edge.

More specifically, Henman's serve was also essential to his memorable triumph. Time and again it rescued him, especially in those tie-breaks, although just as importantly, it was also the key when he held from 0-40 in the seventh game of the third set which meant that he, rather than his opponent, would serve first in the fourth at a time when Federer's game was rolling. Also when the Henman serve alone was not good enough to win the point, the follow-up volleys certainly were.

missed a perfectly makeable forehand and then had to save a match point at 5-6, achieved her immediate target of keeping the match alive by racing away with the tie-break 7-1. By now the spectators had flocked back in expectation of a grand climax but it was not to be. Williams stepped up the pressure again and broke twice in establishing a 3-0 lead. Although her serve temporarily wavered again when she double faulted twice to lose the fourth game, the struggling Davenport was still unable to capitalise on the chance she was offered, leaving the 1999 champion to say 'It seemed as if I didn't start any of the sets very well. I wish I knew why. That first game of the final set was huge if I was to keep the momentum going but I didn't get it and that lifted her confidence once more.'

What followed on Centre Court was a hilarious 35-and-over invitation doubles in which that unrivalled master of trick shots Mansour Bahrami and Henri Leconte, his eager partner in comic looks and lunges, eventually lost 7-5 6-4 to Sergio Casal and Emilio Sanchez. The Spaniards were happy to play the straight men until they felt it was time to show who were the bosses. The crowd revelled in the fun, especially when Bahrami and Leconte sat in the sideline officials' chairs and bounced their way forward for each successive return until they were actually at the baseline — and still playing.

In the absence of Mark Woodforde who had retired but was back at The Championships just the same, Todd Woodbridge had teamed up for the year with another well established exponent of the doubles art, Jonas Bjorkman but there was not to be another title for the Australian. He and the experienced Swede had been beaten in the third round by Bob and Mike Bryan and, on this day, it was the hopes of the 23-year-old Californians which faded. They lost their semi-final on No. 1 Court 6-4 7-6 4-6 6-1, to the higher-seeded Jiri Novak and David Rikl of the

Czech Republic, who were to face Don Johnson and Jared Palmer, 7-6 4-6 7-5 6-3 winners over Max Mirnyi and Vladimir Voltchkov. There was another chance for the Bryan boys for both were still alive in the mixed doubles.

Elena Baltacha and Anne Keothavong remained on course for the first all-British final of the girls' singles when both again combined skill with resilience and willpower in two more three-set matches, to reach their respective quarter finals. Baltacha recovered from being 0-3 and 1-4 and then two points from defeat at 5-6 in the final set to overcome the fourth-seeded Russian, Svetlana Kuznetsova 7-5 6-7 9-7 in 2 hours 44 minutes on No. 2 Court. Meanwhile on No. 3 Court, Keothavong showed equal resolve and spirit as she shrugged off a thigh strain and the loss of the first set by serving out for a 3-6 7-6 7-5 victory at the second attempt over another of the crop of emerging Russians, Anna Bastrikova.

Not such British joy in the boys' event for qualifier Ken Skupski, who had exceeded all expectations, including his own, by reaching the quarter finals but was then eliminated 6-2 7-6 by Germany's Philipp Petzschner.

Left: The scoreboard shows that the supremely athletic Venus Williams is on the point of repeating her final victory the previous year against Lindsay Davenport (above).

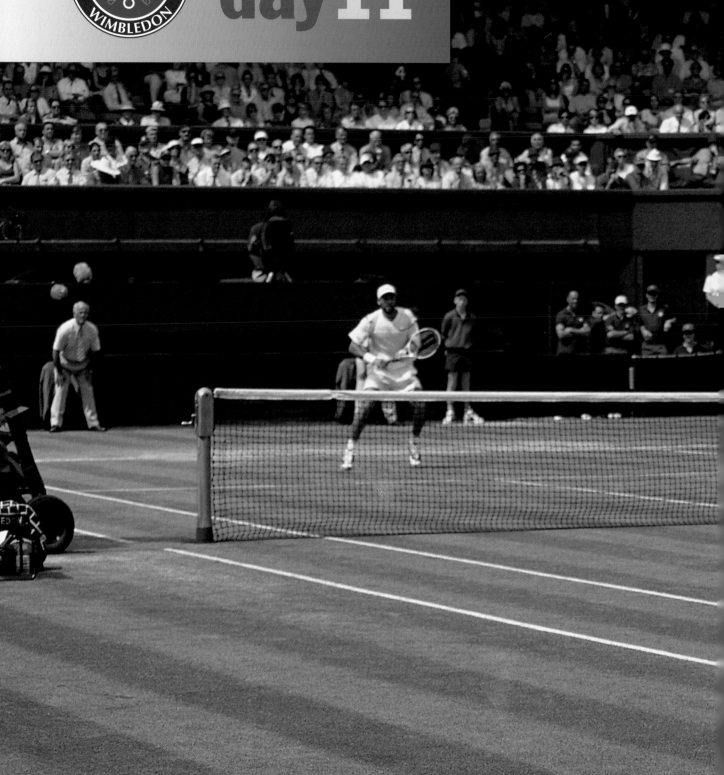

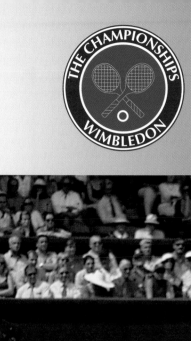

Previous page: Pat Rafter (left) and
Andre Agassi in another classic semi-
final encounter.

**Above: British umpire, Mike Morrissey,
also needed to quench his thirst during
the changeovers.**

It was cruelly ironic that the first major
weather interruption of Wimbledon
2001 came just as Tim Henman looked
set to achieve part one of his personal
dream by reaching the men's singles
final.

Having fought his way back from losing an opening set which had been won
by a three-gun barrage of wonderful returns by Goran Ivanisevic in the 12th
game to be leading by two sets to one
and 2-1, the black cloud which had been
hovering menacingly to the east of the
All England Club for an hour, finally
edged its way over the Centre Court.

At 6.18 pm, after almost two hours
of play, the covers came on. Two hours
later play was abandoned for the day,
leaving both players and the crowd in a
state of nervous limbo. The rain could
not have come at a worse time for Henman, who was looking so tantalisingly
close to becoming the first British man
since Bunny Austin, 63 years earlier, to
reach the final.

It is a familiar cliché in tennis that a
match is never won until the last point
has been played. That is the beauty of
the game's scoring system and the delay
meant that although Henman had
seemed to be in control after Ivanisevic
lost two mini-breaks in the second set
tie-break, the Croat would have had
ample time to get his head together
again by the time they resumed the following afternoon.

Meanwhile Pat Rafter was already
through to the final for a second year in
succession after snatching a 2-6 6-3 3-6
6-2 8-6 victory over Andre Agassi in an
earlier contest while the sun was still
shining. The match was almost as consistently gripping as their semi-final a
year earlier, when the Australian was also
victorious.

It was because there had been such a
nail-biting finish to the Rafter–Agassi
clash that the Centre Court was only
about two thirds full by the time Ivanisevic slammed down four enormous serves
in the opening game to set the tone for
the first set.

The steadfast Henman against the
charismatic Ivanisevic was always going
to be a battle for supremacy between the
Croat's booming serves — 150 of which
had already been aces in his previous five
rounds — and the quality of Henman's
returns. As it happened Henman, who
managed to return only one of his opponent's first four serves into court, struck
the first ace but it was not long before
more of the same were rolling regularly
from his opponent's racket, most importantly to snatch back the home player's
first break point in the fifth game. As
usual Ivanisevic asked for the same ball
back to try and repeat the magic on the
next point and there were was roar of
laughter from the crowd when instead
he hit a fault.

Henman was sensibly trying to whip
up noisy support from the crowd but
they were shocked into comparative si-
lence for a while after their man hit an
ace on the first point at 5-6 but was then
rocked by a series of the most spectacular
returns by Ivanisevic, culminating in a
set-winning backhand service return
down the line.

The first real chance for Henman
came at 4-4 in the second set when
Ivanisevic, the first wild-carded player to
go so far in the men's singles, double
faulted twice in succession to 15-40.
Henman's backhand was a shade long on
the first of the break points. Ivanisevic,
though, escaped the second and, two
points later, a third by demonstrating
once again his ability to hit aces so often
when facing such potential peril.

It might have been enough to weaken
the resolve of some players; but not
Henman. Instead he remained focused,
constantly searching for ways to increase
the pressure in the hope that his opponent might weaken. Three brilliant volleys when he was serving at 5-6 made
sure of a tie-break to the end of the second set where Ivanisevic's failure to capitalise on two mini-breaks not only cost
him the set but spectacularly changed
the balance of the match.

From being so close to going two sets

Goran Ivanisevic (left) knew he was staring defeat in the face when he lost the third set 6-0 against a rampant Tim Henman but then the rain came to his rescue and the covers came on, making it a frustrating end to the day for the British number one.

down, Henman raced away with the third set 6-0 in a fraction under 15 minutes, while the three-times former finalist continued to fret in particular about the collapse of his volleying confidence at a time when his opponent's volleying had never been sharper.

Henman dropped only four points in the third set, completing it with another of his tormenting lobs but moments after he had escaped injury when sliding into the umpire's chair early in the fourth set the weather meant that the wait, which for British tennis had seemed never-ending, would last at least another day.

Rafter's hopes of staying alive had looked remote when Agassi, who had looked the better player throughout, stepped up to serve for the match at 5-4 in the final set. Yet at 30-40 Rafter, who had not been allowed to dictate from the net as much as he had hoped or needed to do, created a vital chance to sneak forward. His high backhand volley earned him a break point and once more he took the risk of following in behind his return and was able to put away a forehand volley.

Suddenly the momentum switched although Rafter still had to stave off a set point at 6-6 which would have left Agassi serving for the match. Instead Rafter held and it was at that point that a line-umpire reported Agassi for a verbal obscenity for which he was later fined $2,000. In next to no time, the irate American, who seemed to think that because hardly anyone heard him it should not have mattered and was clearly distracted, slipped to 0-40. He saved the first two match points, the first with a typically explosive backhand down the line, but Rafter's hooked backhand pass on the third was a winner.

'I can't believe it, I'm very lucky' said Rafter. 'He was definitely the better player. For me the turning point was when I escaped from 15-40 at 0-2 in the final set. He had a pretty easy forehand but I guessed the right way. I knew that

if I had lost that game the game was over' added the Australian who said he 'felt bad for Andre because I thought he was unlucky with a couple of line calls.' In fact television replays showed that both those calls were correct.

While Justine Henin was preparing for her ladies' singles final the following

day against defending champion, Venus Williams, her compatriot, Kim Clijsters underlined the growing strength of tennis in Belgium by reaching her second final in as many years. In 2000 she had

A disappointed Steffi Graf (inset) looks on
as her defeated boyfriend congratulates
Pat Rafter on beating him again in the
semi-final.

partnered her boyfriend, Lleyton Hewitt to the mixed doubles final. This time, her occasional partnership with the highly capable Japanese doubles player, Ai Sugiyama, was also strong enough to reach the final of the ladies' doubles when they upset the French Open champions from Spain and Argentina, Virginia Ruano Pascual and Paolo Suarez, 6-4 6-4.

The other semi-final went according to form with the top seeds, Lisa Raymond of the United States and Rennae Stubbs of Australia, comfortably beating fifth seeds Kimberley Po-Messerli of the United States and Nathalie Tauziat, for whom it was a final Wimbledon appearance, 6-3 7-5.

Meanwhile there was high drama on Court 18 in the quarter final of the mixed doubles where fourth seeds, Mahesh Bhupathi from India and the Russian, Elena Likhovtseva, were stretched to a marathon 15-13 final set by the unseeded pairing of Bob Bryan and Lisa McShea. They had been rained off the previous night at 5-4 in the final set but as the pressure mounted, it was Bhupathi's extra experience — he won the men's doubles title with Leander Paes two years earlier — which proved decisive as he and his partner prevailed 6-1 4-6 15-13.

Waiting for them were Bryan's twin brother, Bob, who had teamed up with South African, Lisa McShea, to beat her fellow countryman, Ellis Ferreira and Sugiyama 6-3 6-2.

Hopes of an all-British final in the girls' singles ended when both Middlesex teenagers, Elena Baltacha and Anne Keothavong were beaten in their respective semi-finals by talented opponents from Indonesia and Russia. The powerfully built Baltacha played well for the most part but paid heavily for a disappointing tie-break as she was beaten 5-7 7-6 6-2 on Court Three by Angelique Widjaja. She won only one of the first seven points in the tie-break and thereafter her challenge faded. Keothavong was outplayed 6-2 6-1 in 54 minutes on Court One by Dinara Safina, sister of the men's singles third seed, Marat Safin.

British interest in the girls' doubles also ended when Cristelle Grier, the daughter of Wimbledon championships director, Richard Grier and her partner, Julia Smith, bowed out in the quarter finals 7-5 6-1 against the more experienced third seeds, Gisela Dulko of Argentina and the outstanding American prospect, Ashley Harkleroad.

Main picture: The Pimms tent and other catering outlets were kept busy in the hot weather.

THE CHAMPIONSHIPS WIMBLEDON

T. HEN

G. IVANI

Ansa

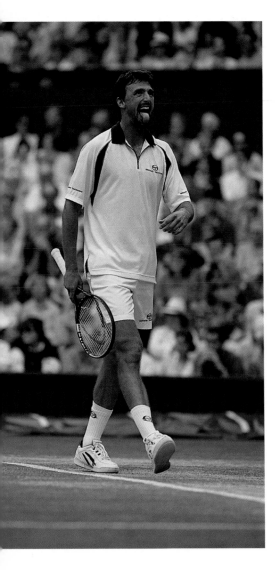

Above: 'How could I have missed that one?' asked Goran Ivanisevic, as the tension began to show in his match with Tim Henman.

...And so it went on. Only 51 minutes' play was possible on Day 12. The finalists for the ladies' singles, defending champion, Venus Williams and Justine Henin, were left kicking their heels until eventually the match was postponed until the following day. Members of the Belgian royal family, their Prime Minister and former U.S. president, Bill Clinton, could only sit and watch the rain for most of the day, like everyone else, and the Henman–Ivanisevic semi-final again remained undecided.

The morning had been ominously cloudy, though mainly dry. Yet just after midday, not long before the British hero and the rejuvenated Croat were due to resume a contest which had been suspended overnight, that infuriating light drizzle which has become all too common over Wimbledon during The Championships fortnight in recent years, once more started to fall.

Despite occasional optimistic announcements from Christopher Gorringe, Chief Executive of the All England Club that they hoped play could begin 15 minutes after the rain stopped, it never quite did. Then just when many in the media rooms were beginning to despair of ever seeing a ball hit on the day, though not the great tennis public which never wants to give up, the sun which had been shining for hours little more than 20 miles away, suddenly broke through meekly over SW 19. At last, at 5.30 pm, the players appeared and eight minutes later Ivanisevic hit an ace, his 18th of the match, to hold his service game which had been interrupted at 40-30 overnight, to make it 2-2 in the fourth set.

The Centre Court was filled to capacity and the first of many huge roars on what was again to be an abbreviated day, greeted an ace also from Henman on his opening service point. The first real tension came in the eighth game when Ivanisevic double faulted to give the British player a break point but the volleying which had let him down so badly in the third set, regained some of its authority as he followed in behind his serve to make it deuce and eventually hold.

Three games later Henman was the one facing a crisis. His backhand volley under pressure made it 15-40 but he served his way to safety and the set moved on to a tie-break, though not before Ivanisevic had played arguably the most sensational shot of the fortnight in the 11th game. He slipped as he moved to make a return but still managed to hit a forehand winner while on his knees. The tie-break started well for Henman. He led 3-1 but lost the fifth point on serve in the middle of four points for Ivanisevic, the most crucial of which was a crunching return which Henman could not cope with and gave Goran a 5-3 lead.

Ivanisevic then fluffed another volley on the tenth point to make it 5-5, but slammed down an ace to reach set point and moments later was celebrating after yet another winning serve return which carried the match into a fifth set just as more drizzle was beginning to fall. It eased again for a while but at 6.29 pm on the clock, with Ivanisevic leading 3-2 on serve and Henman serving at 30-15, everyone had to take cover again.

After consultations with both players and Pat Rafter, already through to the final, it was decided that, although a third attempt would be made to complete the match the following day, followed by the delayed ladies' singles final, the winner between the British number one and the Croat would not face the Australian for the title until a day later, the third Monday.

It presented major operational problems for the tournament but was seen as the fairest solution for all concerned. Although Stefan Edberg did not complete his 1988 victory over Boris Becker in the final until the third Monday after only five games had been possible on the Sunday, Wimbledon 2001 would present the first men's singles final to actually start on a third Monday since Gerald Patterson beat Randolph Lycett in 1922 — the tournament's inaugural year at Church Road.

I love the U.S. Open and I was excited by the French Open because of the clay surface and being right there on the court. But this is the greatest tournament in the world. There's nothing like it and everybody knows it. Even people like me who don't play tennis anymore but who love to watch it, we all sit round and wait for Wimbledon every year to see who wins so we know what we're supposed to think about who the greatest tennis players in the world are.

Former U.S. President, Bill Clinton, being interviewed by BBC Sport reporter Garry Richardson for the Centre Court crowd during the lengthy rain delay.

THE CHAMPIONSHIPS WIMBLEDON

Main picture: The lensmen took their photographs of the ladies' finalists with their trophies.

Then it became the turn of the spectators as Venus held the trophy aloft for them.

with a backhand volley underlined her ability and long-term potential.

Williams's loss of the second set, which came about after she had double faulted in the middle of a nervous eighth game, was actually good for the match, as well as for her because it spurred the American into turning up the heat to such an extent that for much of the third set her tennis more than matched anything she had produced earlier in the year.

Once the third set began, power ruled all the way. A break for Williams in the second game was the beginning of the end. A still-defiant Henin saved three of the nine break points she faced during the 68-minute final, one of them when she outpaced and outwitted her opponent in an exhilarating exchange of volleys. Despite the encouragement of a crowd which at times applauded errors by Williams even more than her winners — one felt for no other reason than most of them wanted to 'mother' the youngster — it was a forlorn hope.

Henin acknowledged that the Williams serve had been the key. 'It was unbelievable, so fast and hit with such precision' she said. Then while Williams was taking her bows as a worthy champion who had become only the fourth player in Open tennis history after Billie Jean King, Martina Navratilova and Steffi Graf to make a successful defence of her title, the courageous Henin added 'Mentally she's also still stronger than me. She had the experience that I don't yet have but I'll be back. I will have many many Wimbledons in my career.'

It was a day when nothing seemed to go right for the Belgians. Kim Clijsters, who followed her compatriot on to Centre Court partnering Ai Sugiyama in the final of the ladies' doubles, also had to settle for the runners-up award. A break of the Clijsters serve in the ninth game gave the initiative to the American, Lisa Raymond, and Australian, Rennae Stubbs, the top seeds and strong favourites after the withdrawal of the defending champions, Venus and Serena Williams. They went on to win 6-4 6-3.

Above: Justine Henin receives the runners-up plate from HRH The Duchess of Kent, while the Duke looks on.

Below: Henin manages a brave wave as Williams blows kisses to the crowd.

Right: Christopher Gorringe, chief executive of the All England Club and tournament referee, Alan Mills (below), watch as Venus Williams responds to the crowd's ovation.

Far right: Venus, champion again.

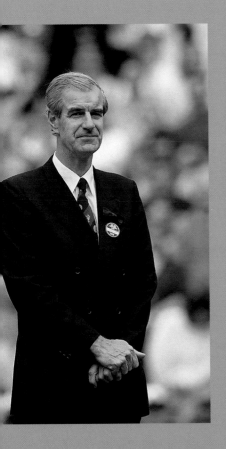

wimbledon • day 13

The men's doubles final which had reached 2-2 in the first set on No. 1 Court during the one short interlude between the rain the night before, suffered another brief interruption from the weather though not enough to alter the general pattern of the match as the Americans, Don Johnson and Jared Palmer, went on to complete a 6-4 4-6 6-3 7-6 victory over the Czech Davis Cup pair, David Rikl and Jiri Novak.

For Rikl, though, the day was not over. He and his Slovakian partner, Karina Habsudova still had to play a semi-final of the mixed doubles, which was effectively settled by a marathon eighth game of the final set when an exhausted Rikl missed a crucial volley. This allowed his fellow countryman, Leos Friedl, to serve out for victory with another Slovakian, Daniela Hantuchova 6-2 5-7 6-3, adding to their surprise 6-2 6-3 win over the holders, Don Johnson and Kimberley Po-Messerli in the quarters. Also through to the final were the unseeded partnership of Mike Bryan and Liezel Huber. The American–South African combination was far too strong for India's Mahesh Bhupathi and the Russian, Elena Likhovtseva, beating them 6-2 6-2.

The new champion in the boys' singles was tenth-seeded Roman Valent, who emulated the Swiss achievement by Roger Federer three years earlier with a 3-6 7-5 6-3 upset victory over second seed, Gilles Muller, the only Luxembourg male player in The Championships. Another piece of Wimbledon history was made in the girls' singles when Angelique Widjaja, seeded eight, became the first Indonesian to win a title. She regained her composure after being outplayed in the second set to beat Marat Safin's sister, Dinara Safina, 6-4 0-6 7-5.

Giovanni Lapentti, no stranger to success at Wimbledon after winning the match-winning Davis Cup rubber for Ecuador against Britain on No. 1 Court almost a year earlier, partnered Frank Dancevic to victory in the boys' doubles when they beat the Mexicans, Bruno Echagaray and Santiago Gonzalez 6-1 6-4 in the final.

Australians dominated the men's seniors events. John Fitzgerald and Wally Masur, now captain and coach respectively to the Australian Davis Cup team, beat the Spaniards, Sergio Casal

and Emilio Sanchez, 7-6 6-0 for the 35-and-over Invitation Doubles, while the 1982 men's doubles champions, Paul McNamee and Pete McNamara took the 45-and-over title with a 6-4 6-3 win over Britain's Colin Dowdeswell and Buster Mottram.

Ros Nideffer retained the ladies' 35-and-over Invitation Doubles though this time with a different fellow South African partner, Ilana Kloss. They beat Britain's Jo Durie and Mima Jausovec of Slovenia, 6-4 5-7 6-3.

day 14 • ivanisevic v rafter

There was a stampede, just like the old days, when the gates were opened for the first-come, first-served crowd on the un-scheduled Day 14. Though instead of charging along the main concourses and diving into the nearest entrances to find the best spots on the Centre Court ter-races, which used to happen before the standing areas were removed as a safety measure, the prize this time for the fastest movers were front-row seats for the men's singles final.

By noon, when Pat Rafter and Goran Ivanisevic walked out, the Cen-tre Court was a colourful mix of Aus-tralian and Croat flags, handmade banners and inflated kangaroos hover-ing precariously in some instances over the heads of those around them. The setting was relentlessly noisy but won-derfully good humoured, prompting Paul Hayward to write in *The Daily*

Telegraph 'This was one of the great tennis stories; one of the best in any sport.' He likened the atmosphere and the match which followed to 'a gladia-torial struggle and the death of English frigidity on the Centre Court. Raucous Australians and Croats turned this manic Monday into a festival for the unfettered spirit.'

Exactly three hours and one minute after Ivanisevic hit a service winner on the opening point — and nine years after he squandered a wonderful oppor-tunity to win the title in his first final — the left-hander at last achieved his life-long dream of becoming Wimbledon champion, in his fourth final.

The wait proved to have been as worthwhile and rewarding for him as it had been for the 13,370 crowd, many of whom had camped out all night to be sure of a ticket and then sustained the

Pat Rafter (above) had no answer to the serve of Goran Ivanisevic (right).

Below: Support for the two finalists was partisan, but friendly.

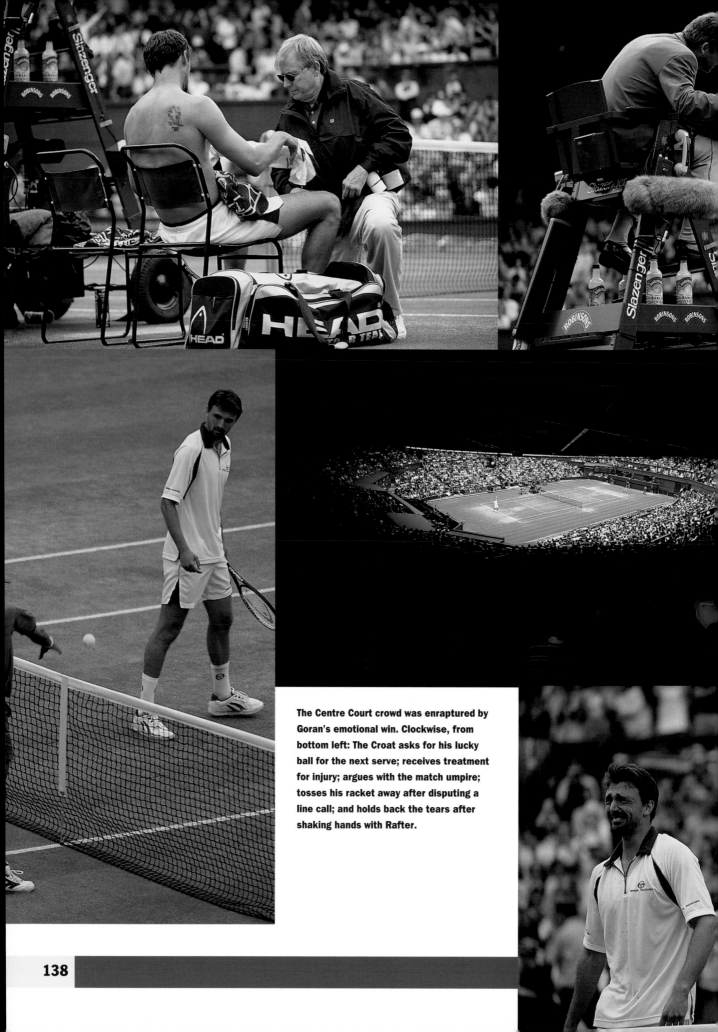

The Centre Court crowd was enraptured by Goran's emotional win. Clockwise, from bottom left: The Croat asks for his lucky ball for the next serve; receives treatment for injury; argues with the match umpire; tosses his racket away after disputing a line call; and holds back the tears after shaking hands with Rafter.

ivanisevic v rafter • day 14

most incredible atmosphere to a match which delivered all that was hoped for and much more in terms of emotion, courage, brilliant tennis and a nail-biting finish.

In years to come, the record books will tell future generations merely that Ivanisevic beat Rafter 6-3 3-6 6-3 2-6 9-7. The scoreline alone though, while hinting at the tantalising twists and turns, hardly begins to convey the tensions and the drama involved. In years to come those lucky enough to have been on Centre Court that day will feel privileged to recall how they had been there when Ivanisevic was not the only one fighting back emotional tears as he nervously double faulted not just on the first match point but also his second before he made it on his fourth.

One of the first to whom he proferred thanks during the presentation ceremony was the All England Club. For without the wild card which gave him the direct entry he needed at a time when his 125 ranking would have directed him only to the qualifying competition at Roehampton, we might have been denied arguably the greatest final day in the 124-year history of The Championships. I can think of one or two greater final matches in both the men's and ladies' singles but in terms of all aspects of a final day, I find it hard to recall one more thrilling and inspiring in my 42 years of reporting The Championships.

No wild-carded players had ever won a Grand Slam and because of the torment Ivanisevic had suffered in the previous two years, fearing that a chronically damaged shoulder might force him to end his career at any moment, the sentimental support for the charismatic left-hander was always going to be enormous. Yet this was a final involving not one but two crowd favourites, one something of a lovable rogue, the other as fine a sportsman you could wish to meet. Indeed Rafter justified all the nice things which had been said about him in his 12 years as one of the finest ambassadors of the sport when, in the midst of his own grim disappointment for the second successive year, he told Ivanisevic at the end 'I'm happy for you, mate.'

One always felt this would be a match settled either by one or two moments of magical inspiration or a careless or tentative shot on a break point. In the first four sets that proved to be the case. The first three were decided by one break in each; the fourth when Ivanisevic was broken twice and on the first occasion, at 2-3, he was close to losing self-control. He was distraught after being foot-faulted on a first serve and he then double faulted down the middle on the second when he was convinced he had hit another ace.

The television replay showed clearly that, as is the case more often than not, the line-umpire had been correct. But having thrown down his racket, kicked the net and been lucky that none of the officials spotted him spitting in the direction of the lady line-umpire who had foot-faulted him, he calmed down to ensure that there was still everything to play for going into the fifth.

No one, surely, could have prescripted the way it went. Having broken Ivanisevic twice in the fourth set so that he was serving first in the decisive fifth, Rafter appeared to have gained the psychological edge. As the pressure mounted, though, he was the one first in danger. His constant serve-and-volley style meant the Australian was always taking the risk of presenting Ivanisevic with a passable target. For the most part Rafter's brave, lunging volleys, not least when he played himself clear of peril with amazing coolness at 4-4 0-30, kept his opponent at bay.

By now also, there was enthusiasm bordering on bedlam at every change-over, as the crowd, which had played its full part in making this such a special occasion, became caught up in the tension. As the pressure mounted, so did the quality of the tennis, with Rafter still producing stunning volleys and

Mine at last! At a time when it looked as if his career was fading into obscurity and retirement, Goran Ivanisevic used his wild card to bounce right back to the top by winning the trophy he had coveted so much for so long.

Ivanisevic stupendous serves when they were most needed.

At 6-7 Ivanisevic was three times two points from defeat. At that moment he showed nerves of steel but two games later with the title beckoning after he had broken Rafter to 15 with two more glorious passes, it was all he could do to hold himself together. In his anxiety to get it finished, he double faulted to 15-30 and did so again at 40-30 after earning his first match point with his 27th ace of the day and his record 213th for the tournament.

The suspense was unbearable. Another winning serve carried Ivanisevic to a second match point. Incredibly overeagerness led to him going for too much on another second serve and double faulting again. A fantastic Rafter lob saved a third match point but on the fourth the Australian at last yielded with a backhand return into the net. Ivanisevic lay face down on the turf for a few seconds before racing over to family and friends as his wild celebrations began.

'I don't know if Wimbledon had seen anything like it. I don't know if they will again' said Ivanisevic, whose abiding memory of the moment will be of 'everybody going nuts'. Almost three hours later several hundred Ivanisevic supporters were still doing precisely that, waiting to cheer a by-now bare-chested Ivanisevic every time they spotted him crossing the bridge between the locker rooms and the players' garden where the champagne was flowing.

In the meantime the other loose ends had been cleared up. Leos Friedl of the Czech Republic and Slovakia's Daniela Hantuchova had been beating the United States–South African partnership of Mike Bryan and Liezel Huber 4-6 6-3 6-2 to take the mixed doubles title, while in the girls' doubles final, Gisela Dulko of Argentina and the American, Ashley Harkleroad, beat Christina Horiatopoulos from Australia and Bethanie Mattek of the United States 6-3 6-1.

So ended Wimbledon 2001, a day later than planned but ultimately none the worse for that for it had the men's singles final which had everything... except, perhaps, the one thing above all many had been hoping for when the tournament began — a British player in line for the title for the first time in 63 years.

Above: Rafter leaves the court to a standing ovation having more than played his part in a classic match.

Left: Goran climbs into the players' box to embrace his family.

Right: Gisela Dulko and Ashley Harkleroad, winners of the girls' doubles.

The Ladies' Singles Championship

Venus Williams

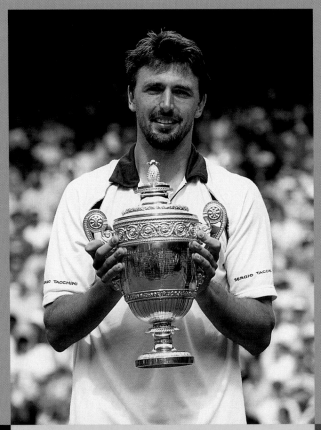

The Gentlemen's Doubles Championship

Donald Johnson & Jared Palmer

The Mixed Doubles Championship

Leos Friedl & Daniela Hantuchova

The Ladies' Doubles Championship

Lisa Raymond & Rennae Stubbs

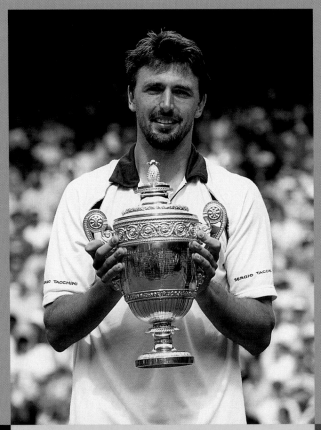

144 **The Gentlemen's Singles Championship**

Goran Ivanisevic

The 35 and over Ladies' Invitation Doubles

Rosalyn Nideffer & Ilana Kloss

The Girls' Doubles Championship

Gisela Dulko & Ashley Harkleroad

The Boys' Doubles Championship

Giovanni Lapentti & Frank Dancevic

The Girls' Singles Championship

Angelique Widjaja

The Boys' Singles Championship

Roman Valent

The 45 and over Gentlemen's Invitation Doubles

Paul McNamee & Peter McNamara

The 35 and over Gentlemen's Invitation Doubles

Wally Masur & John Fitzgerald

CHAMPIONSHIP RECORDS 2001

ALPHABETICAL LIST OF COMPETITORS

LADIES

- **60** Ahl Miss L.A. *(Great Britain)*
- Arendt Miss N. *(USA)*
- **127** Asagoe Miss S. *(Japan)*
- Augustus Miss A. *(USA)*
- **100** Bacheva Miss L. *(Bulgaria)*
- Bachmann Miss A. *(Germany)*
- **85** Baltacha Miss E. *(Great Britain)*
- **70** Barna Miss A. *(Germany)*
- **27** Basting Miss Y. *(Netherlands)*
- Basuki Miss Y. *(Indonesia)*
- **10** Bedanova Miss D. *(Czech Republic)*
- Bes Miss E. *(Spain)*
- **103** Black Miss C. *(Zimbabwe)*
- **29** Boogert Miss K. *(Netherlands)*
- **52** Bovina Miss E. *(Russia)*
- **18** Bradshaw Miss A. *(USA)*
- **58** Brandi Miss K. *(USA)*
- **102** Buth Miss D. *(USA)*
- **12** Cacic Miss S. *(USA)*
- Callens Miss E.S.H. *(Belgium)*
- **33** Capriati Miss J. *(USA)*
- **6** Carlsson Miss A. *(Sweden)*
- **66** Casoni Miss G. *(Italy)*
- **94** Castano Miss C. *(Colombia)*
- **101** Cervanova Miss L. *(Slovak Republic)*
- **20** Chladkova Miss D. *(Czech Republic)*
- **65** Clijsters Miss K. *(Belgium)*
- **80** Coetzer Miss A.J. *(South Africa)*
- **77** Collin Miss H. *(Great Britain)*
- Courtois Miss L. *(Belgium)*
- **122** Craybas Miss J. *(USA)*
- Crook Miss H. *(Great Britain)*
- **28** Cross Miss K.M. *(Great Britain)*
- **99** Daniilidou Miss E. *(Greece)*
- **96** Davenport Miss L.A. *(USA)*
- Davies Miss V.E. *(Great Britain)*
- De Lone Miss E.R. *(USA)*
- **82** De Los Rios Miss R. *(Paraguay)*
- De Villiers Miss N. *(South Africa)*
- **86** Dechy Miss N. *(France)*
- **17** Dementieva Miss E. *(Russia)*
- Dhenin Miss C. *(France)*
- **83** Diaz-Oliva Miss M. *(Argentina)*
- **81** Dokic Miss J. *(Yugoslavia)*
- **23** Dominikovic Miss E. *(Australia)*
- **39** Dragomir Ilie Mrs R. *(Romania)*
- **68** Drake Miss M. *(Canada)*
- Dyrberg Miss E. *(Denmark)*
- Ellwood Miss A. *(Australia)*
- Embry Miss J. *(USA)*
- **113** Farina Elia Mrs S. *(Italy)*
- **50** Fernandez Miss C. *(Argentina)*
- **79** Foretz Miss S. *(France)*
- **56** Frazier Miss A. *(USA)*
- Fusai Miss A. *(France)*
- **59** Gagliardi Miss E. *(Switzerland)*
- **115** Garbin Miss T. *(Italy)*
- **114** Gersi Miss A. *(Czech Republic)*
- **61** Glass Miss A. *(Germany)*
- Golarsa Miss L. *(Italy)*
- **69** Grande Miss R. *(Italy)*
- Grandin Miss N. *(South Africa)*
- Grant Miss K. *(South Africa)*
- Guse Miss K-A. *(Australia)*
- **45** Habsudova Miss K. *(Slovak Republic)*
- **126** Hantuchova Miss D. *(Slovak Republic)*
- **32** Henin Miss J. *(Belgium)*
- **1** Hingis Miss M. *(Switzerland)*
- Hiraki Miss R. *(Japan)*
- **84** Hopkins Miss J. *(USA)*
- **24** Huber Miss A. *(Germany)*
- Huber Mrs L. *(South Africa)*
- **109** Husarova Miss J. *(Slovak Republic)*
- **35** Irvin Miss M. *(USA)*
- **30** Jeyaseelan Miss S. *(Canada)*
- Jidkova Miss A. *(Russia)*
- **91** Kandarr Miss J. *(Germany)*
- **53** Keothavong Miss A. *(Great Britain)*
- **51** Kleinova Miss S. *(Czech Republic)*
- Kolbovic Miss R. *(Canada)*
- **3** Krasnoroutskaya Miss L. *(Russia)*
- **57** Kremer Miss A. *(Luxembourg)*
- Krizan Miss T. *(Slovenia)*
- **75** Kruger Miss J. *(South Africa)*
- **63** Kuti Kis Miss R. *(Hungary)*
- **19** Lamade Miss B. *(Germany)*
- **26** Latimer Miss L. *(Great Britain)*
- **54** Lee Miss J. *(Chinese Taipei)*
- **37** Leon Garcia Miss G. *(Spain)*
- **121** Likhovtseva Miss E. *(Russia)*
- **43** Llagostera Miss N. *(Spain)*
- **78** Loit Miss E. *(France)*
- **74** Majoli Miss I. *(Croatia)*
- **49** Maleeva Miss M. *(Bulgaria)*
- **110** Mandula Miss P. *(Hungary)*
- Marosi-Aracama Mrs K. *(Hungary)*
- **76** Marrero Miss M. *(Spain)*
- Martincova Miss E. *(Czech Republic)*
- **9** Martinez Miss C. *(Spain)*
- **118** Martinez Miss M.J. *(Spain)*
- **87** Matevzic Miss M. *(Slovenia)*
- **97** Mauresmo Miss A. *(France)*
- McNeil Miss L.M. *(USA)*
- **47** McQuillan Miss R. *(Australia)*
- McShea Miss L. *(Australia)*
- **92** Medina Garrigues Miss A.I. *(Spain)*
- Miyagi Miss N. *(Japan)*
- **93** Molik Miss A. *(Australia)*
- Montalvo Miss L. *(Argentina)*
- **72** Montolio Miss A. *(Spain)*
- Musgrave Miss T. *(Australia)*
- **42** Myskina Miss A. *(Russia)*
- Nacuk Miss S. *(Yugoslavia)*
- **105** Nagyova Miss H. *(Slovak Republic)*
- Navratilova Miss M. *(USA)*
- **90** Nejedly Miss J. *(Canada)*
- **67** Nola Mrs P. *(New Zealand)*
- **125** Oremans Miss M. *(Netherlands)*
- **13** Osterloh Miss L. *(USA)*
- **40** Panova Miss T. *(Russia)*
- Perebiynis Miss T. *(Ukraine)*
- **119** Petrova Miss N. *(Russia)*
- **38** Pisnik Miss T. *(Slovenia)*
- **31** Pitkowski Miss S. *(France)*
- **117** Plischke Miss S. *(Austria)*
- Po-Messerli Mrs K. *(USA)*
- **11** Poutchek Miss T. *(Belarus)*
- **111** Prakusya Miss W. *(Indonesia)*
- **98** Pratt Miss N.J. *(Australia)*
- **22** Pullin Miss J.M. *(Great Britain)*
- **25** Raymond Miss L.M. *(USA)*
- **71** Razzano Miss V. *(France)*
- **62** Rittner Miss B. *(Germany)*
- **2** Ruano Pascual Miss V. *(Spain)*
- **8** Rubin Miss C. *(USA)*
- **15** Salerni Miss M.E. *(Argentina)*
- **16** Sanchez Vicario Miss A. *(Spain)*
- **88** Schett Miss B. *(Austria)*
- **36** Schiavone Miss F. *(Italy)*
- Schlukebir Miss K. *(USA)*
- **46** Schnitzer Miss M. *(Germany)*
- **89** Schnyder Miss P. *(Switzerland)*
- **7** Schwartz Miss B. *(Austria)*
- Selyutina Miss I. *(Kazakhstan)*
- **120** Serna Miss M. *(Spain)*
- **106** Serra-Zanetti Miss A. *(Italy)*
- **5** Sfar Miss S. *(Tunisia)*
- **73** Shaughnessy Miss M. *(USA)*
- **4** Sidot Miss A-G. *(France)*
- **124** Smashnova Miss A. *(Israel)*
- Srebotnik Miss K. *(Slovenia)*
- **116** Stevenson Miss A. *(USA)*
- Stubbs Miss R.P. *(Australia)*
- **41** Suarez Miss P. *(Argentina)*
- **95** Sucha Miss M. *(Slovak Republic)*
- **44** Sugiyama Miss A. *(Japan)*
- **104** Tanasugarn Miss T. *(Thailand)*
- Tarabini Miss P. *(Argentina)*
- Tatarkova Miss E. *(Ukraine)*
- **112** Tauziat Miss N. *(France)*
- **48** Testud Miss S. *(France)*
- **123** Torrens-Valero Miss C. *(Spain)*
- Trinder Miss N. *(Great Britain)*
- **14** Tu Miss M. *(USA)*
- **108** Tulyaganova Miss I. *(Uzbekhistan)*
- Vaidyanathan Miss N. *(India)*
- **55** Vavrinec Miss M. *(Switzerland)*
- **34** Vento Miss M.A. *(Venezuela)*
- Vis Miss C.M. *(Netherlands)*
- Wartusch Miss P. *(Austria)*
- Webb Miss V. *(Canada)*
- **21** Weingartner Miss M. *(Germany)*
- **64** Williams Miss S. *(USA)*
- **128** Williams Miss V. *(USA)*
- **107** Woodroffe Miss L.A. *(Great Britain)*
- Yoshida Miss Y. *(Japan)*
- Zaric Miss D. *(Yugoslavia)*

GENTLEMEN

- **6** Acasuso J. *(Argentina)*
- Adams D. *(South Africa)*
- **128** Agassi A. *(USA)*
- Albano P. *(Argentina)*
- **89** Arazi H. *(Morocco)*
- Arnold L. *(Argentina)*
- **85** Arthurs W. *(Australia)*
- Aspelin S. *(Sweden)*
- **69** Balcells J. *(Spain)*
- Barnard M. *(South Africa)*
- Behr N. *(Israel)*
- Bertolini M. *(Italy)*
- Bhupathi M. *(India)*
- **9** Bjorkman J. *(Sweden)*
- **58** Black B. *(Zimbabwe)*
- **74** Black W. *(Zimbabwe)*
- Blake J. *(USA)*
- **35** Blanco G. *(Spain)*
- **62** Boutter J. *(France)*
- Bowen D. *(USA)*
- Braasch K. *(Germany)*
- Brandi C. *(Italy)*
- **99** Bruguera S. *(Spain)*
- **28** Bryan B. *(USA)*
- Bryan M. *(USA)*
- **10** Burgsmuller L. *(Germany)*
- **119** Calatrava A. *(Spain)*
- **91** Calleri A. *(Argentina)*
- **71** Canas G. *(Argentina)*
- Capriati S. *(USA)*
- Carbonell T. *(Spain)*
- **70** Carlsen K. *(Denmark)*
- Carrasco J. *(Spain)*
- Cermak F. *(Czech Republic)*
- **11** Chang M. *(USA)*
- **124** Childs L. *(Great Britain)*
- Cibulec T. *(Czech Republic)*
- **2** Clavet F. *(Spain)*
- **48** Clement A. *(France)*
- Coetzee J. *(South Africa)*
- **121** Coria G. *(Argentina)*
- **3** Cowan B. *(Great Britain)*
- Crichton T. *(Australia)*
- **79** Damm M. *(Czech Republic)*
- Davidson J. *(Great Britain)*
- De Jager J-L. *(South Africa)*
- **125** Delgado J. *(Great Britain)*
- **100** Dent T. *(USA)*
- **31** Derepasko A. *(Russia)*
- **14** Diaz J. *(Spain)*
- **93** Dosedel S. *(Czech Republic)*
- **43** Draper S. *(Australia)*
- **83** Dupuis A. *(France)*
- Eagle J. *(Australia)*
- **102** El Aynaoui Y. *(Morocco)*
- Ellwood B. *(Australia)*
- **108** Elsner D. *(Germany)*
- **80** Enqvist T. *(Sweden)*
- Erlich J. *(Israel)*
- **105** Escude N. *(France)*
- **16** Federer R. *(Switzerland)*
- Ferreira E. *(South Africa)*
- **113** Ferreira W. *(South Africa)*
- **64** Ferrero J.C. *(Spain)*
- **106** Fish M. *(USA)*
- Fisher A. *(Australia)*
- Florent A. *(Australia)*
- Freelove O. *(Great Britain)*
- Friedl L. *(Czech Republic)*
- Fukarek O. *(Czech Republic)*
- **17** Gambill J-M. *(USA)*
- Garcia M. *(Argentina)*
- **72** Gaudio G. *(Argentina)*
- **55** Godwin N. *(South Africa)*
- Goellner M-K. *(Germany)*
- **112** Grosjean S. *(France)*
- **98** Gustafsson M. *(Sweden)*
- **73** Haas T. *(Germany)*
- Haggard C. *(South Africa)*
- Hanley P. *(Australia)*
- Hawk B. *(USA)*
- Haygarth B. *(South Africa)*
- **32** Henman T. *(Great Britain)*
- **52** Heuberger I. *(Switzerland)*
- **97** Hewitt L. *(Australia)*
- Hill M. *(Australia)*
- **4** Hilton M.A. *(Great Britain)*
- **77** Hipfl M. *(Austria)*
- Hood M. *(Argentina)*
- **41** Hrbaty D. *(Slovak Republic)*
- **78** Huet S. *(France)*
- Humphries S. *(USA)*
- **50** Ilie A. *(Australia)*
- **54** Ivanisevic G. *(Croatia)*
- **49** Johansson T. *(Sweden)*
- Johnson D. *(USA)*
- **53** Jonsson F. *(Sweden)*
- **65** Kafelnikov Y. *(Russia)*
- **101** Kempes E. *(Netherlands)*
- **120** Kiefer N. *(Germany)*
- Kilderry P. *(Australia)*
- Kim K. *(USA)*
- Kitinov A. *(Macedonia)*
- **47** Knippschild J. *(Germany)*
- **34** Knowle J. *(Austria)*
- Knowles M. *(Bahamas)*
- Koenig R. *(South Africa)*
- **26** Koubek S. *(Austria)*
- **111** Kratochvil M. *(Switzerland)*
- Kratzmann A. *(Australia)*
- Landsberg J. *(Sweden)*
- Lareau S. *(Canada)*
- **19** Larsson M. *(Sweden)*
- Leach R. *(USA)*
- **38** Lee H-T. *(Korea Republic)*
- **29** Lee M. *(Great Britain)*
- **8** Levy H. *(Israel)*
- **109** Ljubicic I. *(Croatia)*
- **76** Llodra M. *(France)*
- Lopez-Moron A. *(Spain)*
- Luxa P. *(Czech Republic)*
- Macpherson D. *(Australia)*
- MacPhie B. *(USA)*
- **13** Malisse X. *(Belgium)*
- **84** Mamiit C. *(USA)*
- Manta L. *(Switzerland)*
- **75** Mantilla F. *(Spain)*
- **57** Martin A. *(Spain)*
- **24** Martin T. *(USA)*
- **123** Massu N. *(Chile)*
- **126** Medvedev A. *(Ukraine)*
- **122** Meligeni F. *(Brazil)*
- Merklein M. *(Bahamas)*
- **63** Milligan L. *(Great Britain)*
- **86** Mirnyi M. *(Belarus)*
- **56** Moya C. *(Spain)*
- Nargiso D. *(Italy)*
- Nelson J. *(Great Britain)*
- **36** Nestor D. *(Canada)*
- **21** Novak J. *(Czech Republic)*
- O'Brien A. *(USA)*
- Olhovskiy A. *(Russia)*
- Orsanic D. *(Argentina)*
- **107** Paes L. *(India)*
- Pala P. *(Czech Republic)*
- Palmer J. *(USA)*
- **68** Parmar A. *(Great Britain)*
- **59** Pavel A. *(Romania)*
- **116** Pioline C. *(France)*
- **118** Pless K. *(Denmark)*
- **40** Portas A. *(Spain)*
- **30** Pozzi G. *(Italy)*
- **37** Prinosil D. *(Germany)*
- **45** Puentes G. *(Spain)*
- **46** Puerta M. *(Argentina)*
- **96** Rafter P. *(Australia)*
- Ram A. *(Israel)*
- Ran E. *(Israel)*
- Rikl D. *(Czech Republic)*
- **7** Robredo T. *(Spain)*
- **15** Rochus C. *(Belgium)*
- **92** Rochus O. *(Belgium)*
- **51** Roddick A. *(USA)*
- Rodriguez M. *(Argentina)*
- Roitman S. *(Argentina)*
- Rosner P. *(South Africa)*
- **20** Rosset M. *(Switzerland)*
- **60** Rusedski G. *(Great Britain)*
- **67** Sa A. *(Brazil)*
- **33** Safin M. *(Russia)*
- **1** Sampras P. *(USA)*
- **90** Sanchez D. *(Spain)*
- **39** Sanguinetti D. *(Italy)*
- **88** Santoro F. *(France)*
- **5** Sargsian S. *(Armenia)*
- **25** Schalken S. *(Netherlands)*
- Schneiter A. *(Italy)*
- **110** Schuettler R. *(Germany)*
- Shimada T. *(Japan)*
- **117** Siemerink J. *(Netherlands)*
- **42** Sluiter R. *(Netherlands)*
- Spencer K. *(Great Britain)*
- Sprengelmeyer M. *(USA)*
- **104** Squillari F. *(Argentina)*
- **23** Srichaphan P. *(Thailand)*
- Stafford G. *(South Africa)*
- Stark J. *(USA)*
- Stepanek R. *(Czech Republic)*
- **114** Stoliarov A. *(Russia)*
- Stolle S. *(Australia)*
- **61** Stoltenberg J. *(Australia)*
- Suk C. *(Czech Republic)*
- **115** Tabara M. *(Czech Republic)*
- Taino E. *(USA)*
- Tarango J. *(USA)*
- Thomas J. *(USA)*
- Tramacchi P. *(Australia)*
- **27** Ulihrach B. *(Czech Republic)*
- Ullyett K. *(Zimbabwe)*
- **95** Vacek D. *(Czech Republic)*
- **94** Vacek J. *(Czech Republic)*
- **12** Vanek J. *(Czech Republic)*
- Vanhoudt T. *(Belgium)*
- **22** Vicente F. *(Spain)*
- **103** Vinciguerra A. *(Sweden)*
- Vizner P. *(Czech Republic)*
- **81** Voltchkov V. *(Belarus)*
- Waite J. *(USA)*
- Wakefield M. *(South Africa)*
- Weiner G. *(USA)*
- Weir Smith J. *(South Africa)*
- **127** Wessels P. *(Netherlands)*
- **44** Woodbridge T.A. *(Australia)*
- **18** Woodruff C. *(USA)*
- **66** Yoon Y-I. *(Korea Republic)*
- **82** Youzhny M. *(Russia)*
- **87** Zabaleta M. *(Argentina)*
- Zimonjic N. *(Yugoslavia)*

GIRLS

- **57** Adamczak Miss M. *(Australia)*
- **20** Argeri Miss M.J. *(Argentina)*
- **24** Arvidsson Miss S. *(Sweden)*
- **32** Baltacha Miss E. *(Great Britain)*
- **58** Barnes Miss A. *(Great Britain)*
- **9** Bartoli Miss M. *(France)*
- **59** Bastrikova Miss A. *(Russia)*
- **34** Bercek Miss D. *(Yugoslavia)*
- **49** Birnerova Miss E. *(Czech Republic)*
- **27** Blow Miss A. *(Great Britain)*
- **63** Brattchikova Miss N. *(Russia)*
- Broome Miss H. *(Great Britain)*
- **37** Casanova Miss D. *(Switzerland)*
- **12** Casanova Miss M. *(Switzerland)*
- **26** Cetkovska Miss P. *(Czech Republic)*
- **46** Chuang Miss C-J. *(Chinese Taipei)*
- Cochran Miss T. *(USA)*
- **10** Devidze Miss S. *(Georgia)*
- **33** Dulko Miss G. *(Argentina)*
- **21** Etienne Miss N. *(Haiti)*
- **5** Farid Miss Y. *(Egypt)*
- **40** Gallovits Miss E. *(Romania)*
- **51** Gerards Miss M. *(Netherlands)*
- **47** Grier Miss C. *(Great Britain)*
- **1** Harkleroad Miss A. *(USA)*
- Hawkins Miss A. *(Great Britain)*
- **23** Horiatopoulos Miss C. *(Australia)*
- **22** Hsieh Miss S-W. *(Chinese Taipei)*
- **52** Jackson Miss J. *(USA)*
- **38** Janaskova Miss E. *(Czech Republic)*
- **64** Jankovic Miss J. *(Yugoslavia)*
- **56** Keothavong Miss A. *(Great Britain)*
- **44** Kix Miss D. *(Austria)*
- **14** Kolb Miss A. *(Germany)*
- **17** Kuznetsova Miss S. *(Russia)*
- **7** Laine Miss E. *(Finland)*
- **28** Liu Miss A. *(USA)*
- Llewellyn Miss R. *(Great Britain)*
- **62** Lopez Miss L. *(Mexico)*
- **42** Lopez-Herrera Miss M-J. *(Mexico)*
- Luzanska Miss T. *(Israel)*
- **39** Mattek Miss B. *(USA)*
- **25** Mezak Miss M. *(Croatia)*
- **61** Migliarini De Leon Miss L. *(Uruguay)*
- **35** Mirza Miss S. *(India)*
- **3** Mortello Miss G. *(Italy)*
- **29** Nociarova Miss D. *(Slovak Republic)*
- **55** O'Brien Miss K. *(Great Britain)*
- **6** O'Donoghue Miss J. *(Great Britain)*
- **15** Peng Miss S. *(China P.R.)*
- Penkova Miss M. *(Bulgaria)*
- **43** Pitts Miss N. *(USA)*
- **30** Rao Miss S. *(USA)*
- **41** Safina Miss D. *(Russia)*
- **19** Sakowicz Miss J. *(Poland)*
- **48** Schaul Miss C. *(Luxembourg)*
- **11** Schiechtl Miss C. *(Austria)*
- **36** Smith Miss J. *(Great Britain)*
- **31** Smolenakova Miss L. *(Slovak Republic)*
- **45** Stosur Miss S. *(Australia)*
- **8** Strycova Miss B. *(Czech Republic)*
- **54** Tognetti Miss L. *(Italy)*
- **4** Torres Miss M. *(Mexico)*
- **18** Valdes Miss E. *(Mexico)*
- Van Boekel Miss D. *(Netherlands)*
- **13** Van Niekerk Miss M. *(South Africa)*
- **2** Voskoboeva Miss G. *(Russia)*
- **60** Vrljic Miss A. *(Croatia)*
- Webley-Smith Miss E. *(Great Britain)*
- **50** Werner Miss S. *(Germany)*
- **16** Widjaja Miss A. *(Indonesia)*
- **53** Zika Miss J. *(Austria)*

BOYS

- **32** Abougzir Y. *(USA)*
- Adjei-Darko H. *(Ghana)*
- **3** Amritraj P. *(USA)*
- Amritraj S. *(USA)*
- **43** Auradou M. *(France)*
- **47** Baghdatis M. *(Cyprus)*
- **4** Baker B. *(USA)*
- **27** Balleret B. *(France)*
- **12** Banks A. *(Great Britain)*
- **53** Bayer M. *(Germany)*
- Berdych T. *(Czech Republic)*
- Blair R. *(South Africa)*
- **42** Bloomfield R. *(Great Britain)*
- **52** Bogdanovic A. *(Great Britain)*
- **41** Bohli S. *(Switzerland)*
- **14** Brewer D. *(Great Britain)*
- **18** Brizzi A. *(Italy)*
- **24** Capdeville P. *(Chile)*
- Chadaj A. *(Poland)*
- **46** Chu J. *(USA)*
- **50** Cohen J. *(USA)*
- **26** Cruciat A. *(Romania)*
- **48** Dabul B. *(Argentina)*
- **21** Dancevic F. *(Canada)*
- **30** De Gier B. *(Netherlands)*
- **15** Durek R. *(Australia)*
- **17** Echagaray B. *(Mexico)*
- **38** Egger M. *(Austria)*
- **11** Emery M. *(USA)*
- **35** Evans C. *(Great Britain)*
- **49** Falla Ramirez A. *(Colombia)*
- Gabashvili T. *(Russia)*
- **51** Gonzalez S. *(Mexico)*
- **44** Gregorc L. *(Slovenia)*
- **19** Gronefeld B. *(Germany)*
- **58** Henry R. *(Australia)*
- **62** Heyl H. *(South Africa)*
- **20** Hutchins R. *(Great Britain)*
- Ivanov P. *(Russia)*
- **59** Jacobs C. *(South Africa)*
- **13** Johansson C. *(Sweden)*
- **39** Kanev I. *(Bulgaria)*
- **60** Kollerer D. *(Austria)*
- Kovacevic G. *(Australia)*
- **34** Lalji N. *(Great Britain)*
- **55** Lapentti G. *(Ecuador)*
- **23** Lemke F. *(Germany)*
- Letcher C. *(Australia)*
- Loglo K. *(Tonga)*
- **22** Masik J. *(Czech Republic)*
- **33** Mayer F. *(Germany)*
- **28** Melo M. *(Brazil)*
- **61** Mihailovic D. *(Yugoslavia)*
- **54** Morel C. *(France)*
- **64** Muller G. *(Luxembourg)*
- **57** Noviski L. *(Argentina)*
- Olsen J. *(New Zealand)*
- **56** Ouahab L. *(Algeria)*
- **45** Petzschner P. *(Germany)*
- **2** Pocock T. *(Great Britain)*
- **63** Posada O. *(Venezuela)*
- **8** Reid T. *(Australia)*
- Riby B. *(Great Britain)*
- **31** Russell R. *(Jamaica)*
- Salamanca C. *(Colombia)*
- **36** Sipaeya S. *(India)*
- **37** Skupski K. *(Great Britain)*
- **29** Smith M. *(Great Britain)*
- **40** Soderling R. *(Sweden)*
- **10** Stadler S. *(Germany)*
- Thomas G. *(Great Britain)*
- **1** Tipsarvevic J. *(Yugoslavia)*
- **5** Tuksar S. *(Croatia)*
- **25** Valent R. *(Switzerland)*
- **9** Vitullo L. *(Argentina)*
- **16** Wang Y-T. *(Chinese Taipei)*
- **7** Wiespeiner S. *(Austria)*
- **6** Zgaga M. *(Slovenia)*
- Zimmermann J. *(USA)*

Bold figures denote position in Singles Draw

THE GENTLEMEN'S SINGLES CHAMPIONSHIP

Holder: P. Sampras

The winner becomes the holder, for the year only, of the CHALLENGE CUP presented by The All England Lawn Tennis and Croquet Club. The winner receives a silver replica of the Challenge Cup. A silver salver is presented to the runner-up and a bronze medal to each defeated semi-finalist.

First Round

1.	P.Sampras [1]	(USA)
2.	F.Clavet	(ESP)
(W) 3.	B.Cowan	(GBR)
(W) 4.	M.A.Hilton	(GBR)
5.	S.Sargsian	(ARM)
6.	J.Acasuso	(ARG)
7.	T.Robredo	(ESP)
8.	H.Levy [34]	(ISR)
9.	J.Bjorkman [33]	(SWE)
10.	L.Burgsmuller	(GER)
11.	M.Chang	(USA)
12.	J.Vanek	(CZE)
13.	X.Malisse	(BEL)
14.	J.Diaz	(ESP)
15.	C.Rochus	(BEL)
16.	R.Federer [15]	(SUI)
17.	J-M.Gambill [12]	(USA)
18.	C.Woodruff	(USA)
19.	M.Larsson	(SWE)
20.	M.Rosset	(SUI)
21.	J.Novak	(CZE)
22.	F.Vicente	(ESP)
(L) 23.	P.Srichaphan	(THA)
24.	T.Martin [23]	(USA)
25.	S.Schalken [26]	(NED)
26.	S.Koubek	(AUT)
27.	B.Ulihrach	(CZE)
(Q) 28.	B.Bryan	(USA)
(W) 29.	M.Lee	(GBR)
30.	G.Pozzi	(ITA)
(Q) 31.	A.Derepasko	(RUS)
32.	T.Henman [6]	(GBR)
33.	M.Safin [4]	(RUS)
(Q) 34.	J.Knowle	(AUT)
35.	G.Blanco	(ESP)
(Q) 36.	D.Nestor	(CAN)
37.	D.Prinosil	(GER)
38.	H-T.Lee	(KOR)
39.	D.Sanguinetti	(ITA)
40.	A.Portas [25]	(ESP)
41.	D.Hrbaty [22]	(SVK)
42.	R.Sluiter	(NED)
(Q) 43.	S.Draper	(AUS)
(Q) 44.	T.A.Woodbridge	(AUS)
45.	G.Puentes	(ESP)
46.	M.Puerta	(ARG)
47.	J.Knippschild	(GER)
48.	A.Clement [13]	(FRA)
49.	T.Johansson [11]	(SWE)
50.	A.Ilie	(AUS)
51.	A.Roddick	(USA)
(Q) 52.	I.Heuberger	(SUI)
53.	F.Jonsson	(SWE)
(W) 54.	G.Ivanisevic	(CRO)
(Q) 55.	N.Godwin	(RSA)
56.	C.Moya [21]	(ESP)
57.	A.Martin [31]	(ESP)
58.	B.Black	(ZIM)
59.	A.Pavel	(ROM)
60.	G.Rusedski	(GBR)
61.	J.Stoltenberg	(AUS)
62.	J.Boutter	(FRA)
(Q) 63.	J.Milligan	(GBR)
64.	J.C.Ferrero [8]	(ESP)
65.	Y.Kafelnikov [7]	(RUS)
(Q) 66.	Y-I.Yoon	(KOR)
67.	A.Sa	(BRA)
(W) 68.	A.Parmar	(GBR)
69.	J.Balcells	(ESP)
70.	K.Carlsen	(DEN)
71.	G.Canas	(ARG)
72.	G.Gaudio [32]	(ARG)
73.	T.Haas [17]	(GER)
(L) 74.	W.Black	(ZIM)
75.	F.Mantilla	(ESP)
(Q) 76.	M.Llodra	(FRA)
77.	M.Hipfl	(AUT)
(Q) 78.	S.Huet	(FRA)
79.	M.Damm	(CZE)
80.	T.Enqvist [10]	(SWE)
81.	V.Voltchkov [16]	(BLR)
82.	M.Youzhny	(RUS)
83.	A.Dupuis	(FRA)
(Q) 84.	C.Mamiit	(USA)
85.	W.Arthurs	(AUS)
86.	M.Mirnyi	(BLR)
87.	M.Zabaleta	(ARG)
88.	F.Santoro [20]	(FRA)
89.	H.Arazi [27]	(MAR)
90.	D.Sanchez	(ESP)
91.	A.Calleri	(ARG)
92.	O.Rochus	(BEL)
93.	S.Dosedel	(CZE)
(L) 94.	J.Vacek	(CZE)
95.	D.Vacek	(CZE)
96.	P.Rafter [3]	(AUS)
97.	L.Hewitt [5]	(AUS)
98.	M.Gustafsson	(SWE)
99.	S.Bruguera	(ESP)
(Q) 100.	T.Dent	(USA)
101.	E.Kempes	(NED)
102.	Y.El Aynaoui	(MAR)
103.	A.Vinciguerra	(SWE)
104.	F.Squillari [28]	(ARG)
105.	N.Escude [24]	(FRA)
(L) 106.	M.Fish	(USA)
(Q) 107.	L.Paes	(IND)
108.	D.Elsner	(GER)
109.	I.Ljubicic	(CRO)
110.	R.Schuettler	(GER)
111.	M.Kratochvil	(SUI)
112.	S.Grosjean [9]	(FRA)
113.	W.Ferreira [14]	(RSA)
114.	A.Stoliarov	(RUS)
115.	M.Tabara	(CZE)
116.	C.Pioline	(FRA)
117.	J.Siemerink	(NED)
(W) 118.	K.Pless	(DEN)
119.	A.Calatrava	(ESP)
120.	N.Kiefer [19]	(GER)
121.	G.Coria [29]	(ARG)
122.	F.Meligeni	(BRA)
123.	N.Massu	(CHI)
(W) 124.	L.Childs	(GBR)
(W) 125.	J.Delgado	(GBR)
126.	A.Medvedev	(UKR)
127.	P.Wessels	(NED)
128.	A.Agassi [2]	(USA)

Second Round

- P.Sampras [1] — 6/4 7/6(5) 6/4
- B.Cowan — 6/3 6/2 7/6(2)
- S.Sargsian — 6/3 6/1 6/4
- T.Robredo — 7/6(5) 6/5 Ret'd
- J.Bjorkman [33] — 6/4 6/3 6/4
- M.Chang — 6/2 6/2 6/7(4) 4/6 6/2
- X.Malisse — 6/2 6/3 6/3
- R.Federer [15] — 6/2 6/3 6/3
- C.Woodruff — 6/4 3/6 6/7(4) 6/3 6/2
- M.Larsson — 6/4 3/6 6/3 1/6 6/2
- J.Novak — 6/1 6/4 6/3
- T.Martin [23] — 6/3 6/4 6/7(4) 6/3
- S.Schalken [26] — 6/4 3/6 6/4 6/7(2) 7/5
- B.Bryan — 6/3 6/4 6/1
- M.Lee — 6/4 6/3 6/1
- T.Henman [6] — 6/1 6/1 6/1
- M.Safin [4] — 6/2 7/5 5/7 6/3
- D.Nestor — 6/2 6/3 6/2
- D.Prinosil — 6/7(5) 6/2 6/4 6/4
- D.Sanguinetti — 6/3 3/6 6/3 6/7(5) 7/5
- R.Sluiter — 6/2 5/7 6/4 6/2
- T.A.Woodbridge — 5/7 6/3 3/6 7/5 6/3
- G.Puentes — 6/3 7/6(2) 6/4
- A.Clement [13] — 7/6(5) 5/7 6/1 6/3
- T.Johansson [11] — 6/4 4/6 6/7(5) 7/6(5) 6/2
- A.Roddick — 6/4 6/4 7/6(0)
- G.Ivanisevic — 6/4 6/4 6/4
- C.Moya [21] — 2/6 6/7(4) 6/3 6/4 6/4
- B.Black — 6/1 6/1 6/0
- G.Rusedski — 7/6(2) 6/7(5) 7/6(1) 6/2
- J.C.Ferrero [8] — 6/2 6/2 6/2
- Y.Kafelnikov [7] — 6/4 6/2 6/4
- A.Parmar — 7/6(3) 6/7(5) 6/4 4/6 8/6
- K.Carlsen — 7/5 7/6(4) 7/6(8)
- G.Canas — 1/6 6/1 3/6 6/2 7/5
- W.Black — 6/4 5/7 6/1 3/0 Ret'd
- F.Mantilla — 6/4 6/2 6/7(5) 3/6 2/1 Ret'd
- S.Huet — 3/6 3/6 6/4 6/4 6/3
- T.Enqvist [10] — 6/1 6/3 7/5
- M.Youzhny — 6/3 6/7(9) 7/6(8) 7/5
- A.Dupuis — 6/4 5/7 6/7(2) 6/3 6/1
- M.Mirnyi — 7/5 6/2 6/4
- F.Santoro [20] — 7/5 6/1 6/3
- H.Arazi [27] — 7/6(4) 6/2 6/3
- O.Rochus — 6/7(5) 6/3 6/3 6/3
- S.Dosedel — 7/5 6/1 1/6 7/6(5)
- P.Rafter [3] — 6/2 7/6(7) 6/3
- L.Hewitt [5] — 6/1 6/2 6/4
- T.Dent — 6/0 6/1 6/4
- Y.El Aynaoui — 7/6(3) 5/7 3/6 6/3 12/10
- A.Vinciguerra — 6/4 7/6(2) 3/6 6/4
- N.Escude [24] — 6/2 6/3 6/2
- L.Paes — 6/0 6/1 3/6 7/5
- R.Schuettler — 7/6(3) 7/6(4) 7/5
- S.Grosjean [9] — 6/3 6/3 6/4
- A.Stoliarov — 7/6(4) 6/3 3/0 Ret'd
- C.Pioline — 6/2 6/3 7/5
- K.Pless — 7/6(5) 6/4 6/4
- N.Kiefer [19] — 2/6 6/3 6/1 6/4
- F.Meligeni — 6/4 3/6 0/6 6/4 6/3
- N.Massu — 6/4 3/6 6/4 7/5
- J.Delgado — 6/2 6/4 7/5
- A.Agassi [2] — 7/6(1) 6/4 6/4

Third Round

- P.Sampras [1] — 6/3 6/2 6/7(5) 4/6 6/3
- S.Sargsian — 6/2 6/4 3/6 6/1
- J.Bjorkman [33] — 7/6(4) 7/6(1) 6/4
- R.Federer [15] — 6/3 7/5 3/6 4/6 6/3
- M.Larsson — 6/4 6/4 6/2
- T.Martin [23] — 6/7(3) 2/6 6/4 6/4 6/4
- S.Schalken [26] — 4/6 6/3 6/4
- T.Henman [6] — 6/2 6/3 6/2
- M.Safin [4] — 7/6(4) 3/6 1/2 Ret'd
- D.Prinosil — 6/3 4/6 6/4 4/6 6/0
- R.Sluiter — 6/4 7/6(3) 2/6 6/3
- A.Clement [13] — 6/3 6/3 6/4
- A.Roddick — 7/6(1) 6/1 4/6 7/6(3)
- G.Ivanisevic — 6/7(5) 6/3 6/4 6/4
- G.Rusedski — 6/1 6/3 6/4
- J.C.Ferrero [8] — 7/6(4) 4/6 6/3 6/7(3) 6/2
- Y.Kafelnikov [7] — 6/7(5) 6/3 6/3 6/1
- G.Canas — 7/5 4/6 6/7(1) 7/6(4) 6/4
- W.Black — 6/1 6/2 7/6(5)
- T.Enqvist [10] — 6/2 7/6(1) 6/1
- M.Youzhny — 7/6(7) 6/3 6/2
- F.Santoro [20] — 7/6(4) 6/1 6/4
- H.Arazi [27] — 7/6(3) 7/6(3) 7/6(3)
- P.Rafter [3] — 7/5 4/6 6/4 6/1
- L.Hewitt [5] — 1/6 7/5 6/3 6/7(2) 6/3
- Y.El Aynaoui — 6/1 6/4 7/6(4)
- N.Escude [24] — 6/3 6/4 6/2
- S.Grosjean [9] — 7/5 6/2 7/6(6)
- A.Stoliarov — 3/6 6/7(3) 6/4 6/3 12/10
- N.Kiefer [19] — 7/6(1) 6/2 6/4
- N.Massu — 6/4 2/6 7/6(2) 6/7(3) 6/4
- A.Agassi [2] — 6/2 6/4 6/3

Fourth Round

- P.Sampras [1] — 6/4 6/4 7/5
- R.Federer [15] — 7/6(4) 6/3 7/6(2)
- T.Martin [23] — 4/6 6/0 6/3 7/5
- T.Henman [6] — 5/7 6/3 6/4 6/2
- M.Safin [4] — 7/6(1) 6/3 5/7 1/6 6/3
- A.Clement [13] — 6/7(4) 7/6(7) 6/4 6/4
- G.Ivanisevic — 7/6(5) 7/5 3/6 6/3
- G.Rusedski — 6/1 6/4 6/4
- Y.Kafelnikov [7] — 6/7(5) 6/3 6/3 6/1
- G.Canas — 3/6 6/1 6/3 7/6(2)
- T.Enqvist [10] — 7/5 6/4 6/2
- M.Youzhny — 7/5 6/0 2/0 Ret'd
- P.Rafter [3] — 7/6(3) 6/4 7/5
- L.Hewitt [5] — 7/5 5/7 6/4 7/6(4)
- N.Escude [24] — 5/7 6/4 6/3 6/4
- A.Agassi [2] — 6/3 6/1 6/1

Quarter-Finals

- R.Federer [15] — 7/6(7) 5/7 6/4 6/7(2) 7/5
- T.Henman [6] — 6/7(3) 7/6(5) 4/6 6/3 6/2
- M.Safin [4] — 6/0 6/3 6/2
- G.Ivanisevic — 7/6(5) 6/4 6/4
- T.Enqvist [10] — 6/3 6/3 6/1
- P.Rafter [3] — 2/6 6/3 6/2 7/5
- N.Escude [24] — 4/6 6/4 3/6 4/6 6/4
- A.Agassi [2] — 6/3 7/5 7/5

(Quarter-final matches)
- T.Henman [6] — 7/5 7/6(6) 2/6 7/6(6)
- G.Ivanisevic — 7/6(2) 7/5 3/6 6/3
- P.Rafter [3] — 6/1 6/3 7/6(5)
- A.Agassi [2] — 6/7(3) 6/3 6/4 6/2

Semi-Finals

- G.Ivanisevic — 7/5 6/7(6) 0/6 7/6(5) 6/3
- P.Rafter [3] — 2/6 6/3 3/6 6/2 8/6

Final

- **G.Ivanisevic — 6/3 3/6 6/3 2/6 9/7**

Heavy type denotes seeded players. The figure in brackets against names denotes the order in which they have been seeded. (W) = Wild card. (Q) = Qualifier. (L) = Lucky loser.

The matches are the best of five sets

Holders: T. A. Woodbridge and M. Woodforde

The winners become the holders, for the year only, of the CHALLENGE CUPS presented by the OXFORD UNIVERSITY LAWN TENNIS CLUB and the late SIR HERBERT WILBERFORCE respectively. The winners receive silver replicas of the two Challenge Cups. A silver salver is presented to each of the runners-up, and a bronze medal to each defeated semi-finalist.

First Round	Second Round	Third Round	Quarter-Finals	Semi-Finals	Final

1. **J.Bjorkman** (SWE) & **T.A.Woodbridge** (AUS) ....[1]
(W) 2. A.Clement (FRA) & N.Escude (FRA) ....
J.Bjorkman & T.A.Woodbridge [1] 6/3 6/2 7/5
3. H.Levy (ISR) & D.Orsanic (ARG) ....
4. T.Crichton (AUS) & P.Rosner (RSA) ....
H.Levy & D.Orsanic ....1/6 4/6 7/6(8) 6/4 6/2
J.Bjorkman & T.A.Woodbridge [1] 6/3 6/4 6/4

(W) 5. B.Cowan (GBR) & J.Delgado (GBR) ....
6. P.Hanley (AUS) & A.Kratzmann (AUS) ....
P.Hanley & A.Kratzmann ....4/6 7/6(10) 6/0 7/6(3)
(W) 7. L.Childs (GBR) & J.Nelson (GBR) ....
8. **B.Bryan** (USA) & **M.Bryan** (USA) ....[15]
B.Bryan & M.Bryan [15] 6/3 6/4 6/4
B.Bryan & M.Bryan [15] ....6/7(1) 6/4 6/1 6/7(3) 6/4

9. **M.Knowles** (BAH) & **B.MacPhie** (USA) ....[11]
10. D.Bowen (USA) & A.Fisher (AUS) ....
M.Knowles & B.MacPhie [11] ....4/6 7/6(4) 6/2 6/2
11. S.Roitman (ARG) & A.Schneiter (ITA) ....
12. J-L.De Jager (RSA) & J.Stark (USA) ....
J-L.De Jager & J.Stark ....6/3 6/3 4/6 6/7(5) 6/2
M.Knowles & B.MacPhie [11] 6/4 6/4 6/4

13. M-K.Goellner (GER) & A.Olhovskiy (RUS) ....
14. M.Damm (CZE) & D.Hrbaty (SVK) ....
M-K.Goellner & A.Olhovskiy 6/3 7/5 3/6 6/4
15. K.Braasch (GER) & J.Knippschild (GER) ....
16. **E.Ferreira** (RSA) & **R.Leach** (USA) ....[5]
E.Ferreira & R.Leach [5] 6/0 6/3 3/6 6/4
E.Ferreira & R.Leach [5] ....7/6(1) 6/4 7/6(4)

17. **J.Novak** (CZE) & **D.Rikl** (CZE) ....[3]
18. M.Garcia (ARG) & D.Nargiso (ITA) ....
J.Novak & D.Rikl [3] 6/4 6/4 1/6 6/2
19. F.Cermak (CZE) & A.Martin (ESP) ....
20. T.Shimada (JPN) & M.Wakefield (RSA) ....
T.Shimada & M.Wakefield ....6/4 6/0 7/6(6)
J.Novak & D.Rikl [3] ....7/6(4) 6/3 7/5

21. E.Taino (USA) & J.Waite (USA) ....
22. A.Kitinov (MKD) & N.Zimonjic (YUG) ....
A.Kitinov & N.Zimonjic ....4/6 7/6(8) 6/4 6/3
23. S.Aspelin (SWE) & J.Landsberg (SWE) ....
24. **S.Humphries** (USA) & **S.Lareau** (CAN) ....[16]
S.Aspelin & J.Landsberg ....6/4 7/6(5) 6/2
A.Kitinov & N.Zimonjic ....7/5 7/6(7) 5/7 6/4

25. **W.Black** (ZIM) & **K.Ullyett** (ZIM) ....[12]
26. T.Cibulec (CZE) & L.Friedl (CZE) ....
T.Cibulec & L.Friedl ....3/6 7/6(4) 6/4
27. N.Behr (ISR) & E.Ran (ISR) ....
28. C.Haggard (RSA) & T.Vanhoudt (BEL) ....
C.Haggard & T.Vanhoudt ....7/6(4) 7/6(2) 6/2
C.Haggard & T.Vanhoudt ....1/6 7/6(9) 2/6 6/0 12/10

29. P.Kilderry (AUS) & P.Tramacchi (AUS) ....
(W) 30. O.Freelove (GBR) & K.Spencer (GBR) ....
P.Kilderry & P.Tramacchi ....7/6(2) 4/6 6/4 6/3
31. D.Adams (RSA) & M.Llodra (FRA) ....
32. **M.Bhupathi** (IND) & **L.Paes** (IND) ....[6]
D.Adams & M.Llodra 6/1 6/3 6/3
D.Adams & M.Llodra 6/2 6/2 6/2

33. **J.Eagle** (AUS) & **A.Florent** (AUS) ....[8]
34. J.Carrasco (ESP) & O.Fukarek (CZE) ....
J.Eagle & A.Florent [8] ....6/2 6/3 5/7 6/7(3) 18/16
35. J.Balcells (ESP) & S.Schalken (NED) ....
36. J.Knowle (AUT) & L.Manta (SUI) ....
J.Balcells & S.Schalken 6/2 6/4 6/3
J.Balcells & S.Schalken ....6/3 7/6(8) 5/7 6/2

37. N.Godwin (RSA) & J.Weir Smith (RSA) ....
38. P.Albano (ARG) & L.Arnold (ARG) ....
P.Albano & L.Arnold 6/4 6/4 1/6 6/3
39. A.Lopez-Moron (ESP) & A.Portas (ESP) ....
40. **D.Prinosil** (GER) & **C.Suk** (CZE) ....[10]
D.Prinosil & C.Suk [10] ....6/3 7/6(5) 6/7(5) 7/5
P.Albano & L.Arnold 0/6 6/4 6/4 5/7 6/4

41. **R.Federer** (SUI) & **W.Ferreira** (RSA) ....[13]
42. J.Coetzee (RSA) & B.Haygarth (RSA) ....
R.Federer & W.Ferreira [13] ....6/7(6) 7/5 6/4 7/5
43. (Q) J.Erlich (ISR) & A.Ram (ISR) ....
44. M.Barnard (RSA) & J.Thomas (USA) ....
J.Erlich & A.Ram ....6/4 6/2 7/6(4)
R.Federer & W.Ferreira [13] 6/3 6/4 7/5

45. M.Bertolini (ITA) & C.Brandi (ITA) ....
46. J.Boutter (FRA) & F.Santoro (FRA) ....
J.Boutter & F.Santoro ....7/6(7) 3/6 2/6 6/7(4) 9/7
47. (Q) J.Blake (USA) & M.Merklein (BAH) ....
48. **D.Johnson** (USA) & **J.Palmer** (USA) ....[4]
D.Johnson & J.Palmer [4] ....6/2 7/6(3) 6/7(7) 6/4
D.Johnson & J.Palmer [4] 3/6 6/1 3/6 6/4 6/2

49. **P.Pala** (CZE) & **P.Vizner** (CZE) ....[7]
50. G.Stafford (RSA) & D.Macpherson (AUS) ....
P.Pala & P.Vizner [7] 6/4 6/4 6/4
51. P.Luxa (CZE) & R.Stepanek (CZE) ....
52. T.Carbonell (ESP) & J.Siemerink (NED) ....
T.Carbonell & J.Siemerink ....6/3 5/7 7/6(5) 6/5
P.Pala & P.Vizner [7] ....6/4 7/5 6/7(5) 7/6(3)

53. M.Hood (ARG) & M.Rodriguez (ARG) ....
54. (Q) K.Kim (USA) & G.Weiner (USA) ....
K.Kim & G.Weiner 6/4 6/4 6/2
(W) 55. M.Lee (GBR) & A.Parmar (GBR) ....
56. **M.Hill** (AUS) & **J.Tarango** (USA) ....[9]
M.Hill & J.Tarango [9] ....7/6(4) 6/7(17) 6/2 6/4
M.Hill & J.Tarango [9] 6/4 4/6 6/3 6/4

57. **B.Black** (ZIM) & **A.O'Brien** (USA) ....[14]
58. W.Arthurs (AUS) & B.Ellwood (AUS) ....
W.Arthurs & B.Ellwood 3/6 2/6 6/3 7/5 6/2
(W) 59. M.Rosset (SUI) & M.Safin (RUS) ....
60. (Q) B.Hawk (USA) & G.Silcock (AUS) ....
M.Rosset & M.Safin ....7/6(4) 6/7(3) 3/6 6/3 10/8
M.Rosset & M.Safin 3/6 3/6 6/3 6/4

61. R.Koenig (RSA) & M.Sprengelmeyer (USA) ....
(W) 62. M.Mirnyi (BLR) & V.Voltchkov (BLR) ....
M.Mirnyi & V.Voltchkov ....6/4 7/6(5) 7/5
63. J-M.Gambill (USA) & A.Roddick (USA) ....
64. **D.Nestor** (CAN) & **S.Stolle** (AUS) ....[2]
D.Nestor & S.Stolle [2] ....6/4 6/3 7/6(1)
M.Mirnyi & V.Voltchkov 3/6 6/2 7/5 6/3

Quarter-Finals:
B.Bryan & M.Bryan [15] ....7/6(1) 7/6(4) 6/3
E.Ferreira & R.Leach [5] ....7/6(2) 6/4 7/6(5)
J.Novak & D.Rikl [3] 6/3 6/3 6/4
C.Haggard & T.Vanhoudt ....6/4 6/7(0) 6/3 2/6 6/3
J.Balcells & S.Schalken ....6/3 4/6 7/6(5) 6/4
D.Johnson & J.Palmer [4] ....w/o
P.Pala & P.Vizner [7] ....6/4 6/7(5) 7/6(2) 6/4
M.Mirnyi & V.Voltchkov ....6/3 7/6(5) 3/6 6/4

Semi-Finals:
B.Bryan & M.Bryan [15] ....6/4 7/6(8) 7/6(5)
J.Novak & D.Rikl [3] ....6/2 6/1 7/6(2)
D.Johnson & J.Palmer [4] ....3/6 6/7(5) 7/6(5) 7/6(6) 6/4
D.Johnson & J.Palmer [4] ....7/6(3) 4/6 7/5 6/3
M.Mirnyi & V.Voltchkov ....7/6(4) 5/7 3/6 6/4 9/7

Semi-Final bracket:
J.Novak & D.Rikl [3] ....6/4 7/6(1) 4/6 6/1

Final:
D.Johnson & J.Palmer [4] ....6/4 4/6 6/3 7/6(6)

149

Heavy type denotes seeded players. The figure in brackets against names denotes the order in which they have been seeded. (W) = Wild card. (Q) = Qualifier. (L) = Lucky loser.

The matches are the best of five sets

THE LADIES' SINGLES CHAMPIONSHIP

Holder: Miss V. Williams

The winner becomes the holder, for the year only, of the CHALLENGE TROPHY presented by The All England Lawn Tennis and Croquet Club. The winner receives a silver replica of the Trophy. A silver salver is presented to the runner-up and a bronze medal to each defeated semi-finalist.

First Round	Second Round	Third Round	Fourth Round	Quarter-Finals	Semi-Finals	Final
1. **Miss M.Hingis [1]** ....(SUI)	Miss V.Ruano Pascual 6/4 6/2					
2. Miss V.Ruano Pascual ....(ESP)		Miss L.Krasnoroutskaya				
3. Miss L.Krasnoroutskaya ....(RUS)	Miss L.Krasnoroutskaya 3/6 6/4 6/2	......................................6/3 7/6(3)				
4. Miss A-G.Sidot ....(FRA)			Miss L.Krasnoroutskaya			
5. Miss S.Sfar ....(TUN)	Miss S.Sfar ....6/7(1) 6/3 6/4		....6/3 6/4			
6. Miss A.Carlsson ....(SWE)		Miss B.Schwartz				
(Q) 7. Miss B.Schwartz ....(AUT)	Miss B.Schwartz ....6/7(1) 6/4 7/5	....6/4 6/4				
8. **Miss C.Rubin [25]** ....(USA)				Miss C.Martinez [19]		
9. **Miss C.Martinez [19]** ....(ESP)	Miss C.Martinez [19] 6/2 3/6 6/3			....6/3 6/4		
10. Miss D.Bedanova ....(CZE)		Miss C.Martinez [19]				
11. Miss T.Poutchek ....(BLR)	Miss S.Cacic 6/3 5/7 6/1	....7/5 6/4				
12. Miss S.Cacic ....(USA)			Miss C.Martinez [19]			
13. Miss L.Osterloh ....(USA)	Miss L.Osterloh 6/4 7/5		....6/2 6/3			
14. Miss M.Tu ....(USA)		Miss L.Osterloh				
15. Miss M.E.Salerni ....(ARG)	Miss A.Sanchez Vicario [13] ...6/3 6/3	....7/6(4) 7/5				
16. **Miss A.Sanchez Vicario [13]** ...(ESP)					Miss J.Henin [8]	
17. **Miss E.Dementieva [10]** ....(RUS)	Miss E.Dementieva [10] 7/5 6/7(9) 6/3				....6/1 6/0	
18. Miss A.Bradshaw ....(USA)		Miss E.Dementieva [10]				
19. Miss B.Lamade ....(GER)	Miss B.Lamade ....6/1 6/7(1) 6/3	....4/6 6/3 6/2				
20. Miss D.Chladkova ....(CZE)			Miss A.Huber [18]			
21. Miss M.Weingartner ....(GER)	Miss M.Weingartner ....3/6 7/6(5) 6/4		....6/0 6/2			
(W) 22. Miss J.M.Pullin ....(GBR)		Miss A.Huber [18]				
23. Miss E.Dominikovic ....(AUS)	Miss A.Huber [18] 6/3 6/2	....7/5 6/1				
24. **Miss A.Huber [18]** ....(GER)				Miss J.Henin [8]		
25. **Miss L.M.Raymond [28]** ....(USA)	Miss L.M.Raymond [28] 6/3 6/0			....4/6 6/2 6/2		
(W) 26. Miss L.Latimer ....(GBR)		Miss L.M.Raymond [28]				
27. Miss Y.Basting ....(NED)	Miss K.M.Cross 6/4 6/4	....6/0 6/1				
(Q) 28. Miss K.M.Cross ....(GBR)			Miss J.Henin [8]			
(Q) 29. Miss K.Boogert ....(NED)	Miss K.Boogert 6/3 6/2		....6/4 7/6(6)			
30. Miss S.Jeyaseelan ....(CAN)		Miss J.Henin [8]				
31. Miss S.Pitkowski ....(FRA)	Miss J.Henin [8] 6/1 6/0	....5/7 7/5 6/2				
32. **Miss J.Henin [8]** ....(BEL)						Miss J.Henin [8]
33. **Miss J.Capriati [4]** ....(USA)	Miss J.Capriati [4] 6/3 6/2					......................2/6 6/4 6/2
34. Miss M.A.Vento ....(VEN)		Miss J.Capriati [4]				
35. Miss M.Irvin ....(USA)	Miss F.Schiavone 2/6 6/1 6/2	....6/3 6/1				
36. Miss F.Schiavone ....(ITA)			Miss J.Capriati [4]			
37. Miss G.Leon Garcia ....(ESP)	Miss T.Pisnik 1/6 6/1 6/4		....6/4 6/4			
38. Miss T.Pisnik ....(SLO)		Miss T.Panova [32]				
39. Mrs R.Dragomir Ilie ....(ROM)	Miss T.Panova [32] 6/3 6/3	....7/6(3) 2/6 6/2				
40. **Miss T.Panova [32]** ....(RUS)				Miss J.Capriati [4]		
41. **Miss P.Suarez [22]** ....(ARG)	Miss A.Myskina ....7/6(5) 6/2			....6/1 6/2		
42. Miss A.Myskina ....(RUS)		Miss A.Sugiyama				
43. Miss N.Llagostera ....(ESP)	Miss A.Sugiyama 7/5 2/6 6/2	....2/6 6/4 6/3				
44. Miss A.Sugiyama ....(JPN)			Miss S.Testud [15]			
45. Miss K.Habsudova ....(SVK)	Miss K.Habsudova 6/1 6/4		....6/7(5) 6/2 6/2			
(Q) 46. Miss M.Schnitzer ....(GER)		Miss S.Testud [15]				
47. Miss R.McQuillan ....(AUS)	Miss S.Testud [15] 6/2 6/2	....6/0 6/1				
48. **Miss S.Testud [15]** ....(FRA)					Miss J.Capriati [4]	
49. **Miss M.Maleeva [12]** ....(BUL)	Miss M.Maleeva [12] 6/0 6/2				....6/7(4) 7/5 6/3	
(Q) 50. Miss C.Fernandez ....(ARG)		Miss M.Maleeva [12]				
51. Miss S.Kleinova ....(CZE)	Miss E.Bovina 3/6 6/2 6/1	....7/5 7/5				
52. Miss E.Bovina ....(RUS)			Miss M.Maleeva [12]			
(W) 53. Miss A.Keothavong ....(GBR)	Miss J.Lee 2/6 6/4 6/3		....6/3 6/2			
(L) 54. Miss J.Lee ....(TPE)		Miss A.Frazier [20]				
55. Miss M.Vavrinec ....(SUI)	Miss A.Frazier [20] 6/1 7/5	....6/4 6/2				
56. **Miss A.Frazier [20]** ....(USA)				Miss S.Williams [5]		
57. **Miss A.Kremer [26]** ....(LUX)	Miss K.Brandi 6/4 6/2			....6/2 6/1		
58. Miss K.Brandi ....(USA)		Miss E.Gagliardi				
59. Miss E.Gagliardi ....(SUI)	Miss E.Gagliardi 6/4 6/1	....6/1 6/2				
(W) 60. Miss L.A.Ahl ....(GBR)			Miss S.Williams [5]			
61. Miss A.Glass ....(GER)	Miss B.Rittner 6/3 6/4		....6/1 6/0			
62. Miss B.Rittner ....(GER)		Miss S.Williams [5]				
63. Miss R.Kuti Kis ....(HUN)	Miss S.Williams [5] 6/1 6/0	....6/4 6/0				
64. **Miss S.Williams [5]** ....(USA)						Miss V.Williams [2]
65. **Miss K.Clijsters [7]** ....(BEL)	Miss K.Clijsters [7] 6/0 6/2					......................6/1 3/6 6/0
66. Miss G.Casoni ....(ITA)		Miss K.Clijsters [7]				
67. Mrs P.Nola ....(NZL)	Miss M.Drake 6/3 6/2	....6/3 6/1				
(Q) 68. Miss M.Drake ....(CAN)			Miss K.Clijsters [7]			
69. Miss R.Grande ....(ITA)	Miss A.Barna 6/4 6/4		....7/5 6/2			
(Q) 70. Miss A.Barna ....(GER)		Miss A.Montolio [27]				
71. Miss V.Razzano ....(FRA)	Miss A.Montolio [27] ....4/6 7/6(5) 6/4	....6/3 6/4				
72. **Miss A.Montolio [27]** ....(ESP)	0/0			Miss K.Clijsters [7]		
73. **Miss M.Shaughnessy [17]** ....(USA)	Miss M.Shaughnessy [17] ....7/6(4) 6/3			....7/6(2) 7/6(5)		
74. Miss I.Majoli ....(CRO)		Miss M.Shaughnessy [17]				
75. Miss J.Kruger ....(RSA)	Miss M.Marrero 4/6 6/3 8/6	....6/0 6/1				
76. Miss M.Marrero ....(ESP)			Miss M.Shaughnessy [17]			
(W) 77. Miss H.Collin ....(GBR)	Miss E.Loit 6/4 6/2		....7/6(4) 2/6 6/1			
78. Miss E.Loit ....(FRA)		Miss A.J.Coetzer [11]				
(Q) 79. Miss S.Foretz ....(FRA)	Miss A.J.Coetzer [11] 6/4 6/4	....6/2 6/3				
80. **Miss A.J.Coetzer [11]** ....(RSA)				Miss L.A.Davenport [3]		
81. **Miss J.Dokic [14]** ....(YUG)	Miss J.Dokic [14] 7/5 6/1			....6/1 6/2		
82. Miss R.De Los Rios ....(PAR)		Miss J.Dokic [14]				
83. Miss M.Diaz-Oliva ....(ARG)	Miss J.Hopkins 3/6 6/3 6/2	....6/2 6/4				
84. Miss J.Hopkins ....(USA)			Miss J.Dokic [14]			
(W) 85. Miss E.Baltacha ....(GBR)	Miss N.Dechy 6/1 7/5		....6/3 7/5			
86. Miss N.Dechy ....(FRA)		Miss B.Schett [21]				
(Q) 87. Miss M.Matevzic ....(SLO)	Miss B.Schett [21] 4/6 6/2 8/6	....7/6(5) 6/3				
88. **Miss B.Schett [21]** ....(AUT)					Miss L.A.Davenport [3]	
89. **Miss P.Schnyder [30]** ....(SUI)	Miss P.Schnyder [30] 6/4 6/4				....7/5 6/4	
90. Miss J.Nejedly ....(CAN)		Miss P.Schnyder [30]				
91. Miss J.Kandarr ....(GER)	Miss J.Kandarr ....6/3 7/6(4)	....6/2 6/2				
92. Miss A.I.Medina Garrigues ....(ESP)			Miss L.A.Davenport [3]			
93. Miss A.Molik ....(AUS)	Miss A.Molik ....6/4 7/6(1)		....6/2 6/3			
94. Miss C.Castano ....(COL)		Miss L.A.Davenport [3]				
95. Miss M.Sucha ....(SVK)	Miss L.A.Davenport [3] 6/3 6/3	....6/4 6/2				
96. **Miss L.A.Davenport [3]** ....(USA)						Miss L.A.Davenport [3]
97. **Miss A.Mauresmo [6]** ....(FRA)	Miss A.Mauresmo [6] ...7/6(6) 4/6 6/4					......................6/2 6/7(1) 6/1
98. Miss N.J.Pratt ....(AUS)		Miss A.Mauresmo [6]				
(Q) 99. Miss E.Daniilidou ....(GRE)	Miss E.Daniilidou 6/0 3/6 6/2	....6/3 6/2				
100. Miss I.Bacheva ....(BUL)			Miss T.Tanasugarn [31]			
101. Miss L.Cervanova ....(SVK)	Miss L.Cervanova 6/2 5/7 6/3		....4/6 6/4			
102. Miss D.Buth ....(USA)		Miss T.Tanasugarn [31]				
103. Miss C.Black ....(ZIM)	Miss T.Tanasugarn [31] ..7/5 6/7(2) 6/3	....6/2 2/6 6/1				
104. **Miss T.Tanasugarn [31]** ....(THA)				Miss N.Tauziat [9]		
105. **Miss H.Nagyova [24]** ....(SVK)	Miss A.Serra-Zanetti ....7/6(4) 6/1			....6/3 6/2		
(Q) 106. Miss A.Serra-Zanetti ....(ITA)		Miss I.Tulyaganova				
(W) 107. Miss L.A.Woodroffe ....(GBR)	Miss I.Tulyaganova ....7/6(5) 6/4	....6/3 6/7(6) 6/2				
108. Miss I.Tulyaganova ....(UZB)			Miss N.Tauziat [9]			
109. Miss I.Husarova ....(SVK)	Miss P.Mandula 0/6 6/2 11/9		....6/0 6/1			
110. Miss P.Mandula ....(HUN)		Miss N.Tauziat [9]				
(Q) 111. Miss W.Prakusya ....(INA)	Miss N.Tauziat [9] 6/4 6/2 0/0	....6/0 6/1				
112. **Miss N.Tauziat [9]** ....(FRA)					Miss V.Williams [2]	
113. **Mrs S.Farina Elia [16]** ....(ITA)	Mrs S.Farina Elia [16] 6/1 6/2				....6/3 6/2	
114. Miss A.Gersi ....(CZE)		Mrs S.Farina Elia [16]				
115. Miss T.Garbin ....(ITA)	Miss A.Stevenson 2/6 6/4 6/4	....6/3 6/2				
(W) 116. Miss A.Stevenson ....(USA)			Miss N.Petrova			
117. Miss S.Plischke ....(AUT)	Miss S.Plischke 6/3 6/4		....6/3 6/3			
118. Miss M.J.Martinez ....(ESP)		Miss N.Petrova				
119. Miss N.Petrova ....(RUS)	Miss N.Petrova 6/3 2/6 6/2	....6/1 6/0				
120. **Miss M.Serna [23]** ....(ESP)				Miss V.Williams [2]		
121. **Miss E.Likhovtseva [29]** ....(RUS)	Miss E.Likhovtseva [29] 6/3 6/4			....6/2 6/0		
122. Miss J.Craybas ....(USA)		Miss E.Likhovtseva [29]				
123. Miss C.Torrens-Valero ....(ESP)	Miss C.Torrens-Valero ....7/6(3) 6/3	....6/1 6/1				
124. Miss A.Smashnova ....(ISR)			Miss V.Williams [2]			
125. Miss M.Oremans ....(NED)	Miss D.Hantuchova ....7/6(2) 7/5		....6/2 6/2			
126. Miss D.Hantuchova ....(SVK)		Miss V.Williams [2]				
127. Miss S.Asagoe ....(JPN)	Miss V.Williams [2] 6/2 6/3	....6/3 6/2				
128. **Miss V.Williams [2]** ....(USA)						

Heavy type denotes seeded players. The figure in brackets against names denotes the order in which they have been seeded. (W) = Wild card. (Q) = Qualifier. (L) = Lucky loser.

The matches are the best of three sets

The winners become the holders, for the year only, of the CHALLENGE CUPS presented by HRH PRINCESS MARINA, DUCHESS OF KENT, the late President of The All England Lawn Tennis and Croquet Club, and The All England Lawn Tennis and Croquet Club. The winners receive silver replicas of the Challenge Cup. A silver salver is presented to each of the runners-up and a bronze medal to each defeated semi-finalist.

First Round	Second Round	Third Round	Quarter-Finals	Semi-Finals	Final

1. **Miss L.M.Raymond** (USA) **& Miss R.P.Stubbs** (AUS) .[1]
2. Miss S.Asagoe (JPN) & Miss Y.Yoshida (JPN) ....
Miss L.M.Raymond & Miss R.P.Stubbs [1] 6/0 7/5
3. Miss R.Hiraki (JPN) & Miss N.Vaidyanathan (IND) ....
4. Mrs S.Farina Elia (ITA) & Miss I.Tulyaganova (UZB) ......
Miss R.Hiraki & Miss N.Vaidyanathan 6/2 6/4

Miss L.M.Raymond & Miss R.P.Stubbs [1] 6/1 6/1

(W) 5. Miss E.Baltacha (GBR) & Miss N.Trinder (GBR) ....
6. Miss E.Bes (ESP) & Miss T.Poutchek (BLR) ....
Miss E.Bes & Miss T.Poutchek 3/6 6/3 6/2
7. Miss N.De Villiers (RSA) & Miss A.Ellwood (AUS) ....
8. **Miss A.J.Coetzer** (RSA) **& Miss L.M.McNeil** (USA) **[14]**
Miss A.J.Coetzer & Miss L.M.McNeil [14] 3/6 6/4 6/3

Miss A.J.Coetzer & Miss L.M.McNeil [14] 1/6 6/2 6/2

Miss L.M.Raymond & Miss R.P.Stubbs [1] 6/2 6/2

9. **Miss T.Garbin** (ITA) **& Miss J.Husarova** (SVK) ....[12]
10. Miss E.R.De Lone (USA) & Miss S.Jeyaseelan (CAN) ......
Miss T.Garbin & Miss J.Husarova [12] 6/3 4/6 6/3
11. Miss L.Courtois (BEL) & Miss L.Krasnoroutskaya (RUS) .
(Q) 12. Miss A.Augustus (USA) & Miss J.Embry (USA) ....
Miss L.Courtois & Miss L.Krasnoroutskaya 6/2 6/1

Miss T.Garbin & Miss J.Husarova [12] 6/2 6/3

Miss I.Majoli & Miss H.Nagyova ......7/6(5) 6/3

13. Miss I.Majoli (CRO) & Miss H.Nagyova (SVK) ....
14. Miss P.Mandula (HUN) & Miss P.Wartusch (AUT) ....
Miss I.Majoli & Miss H.Nagyova 6/4 6/3
15. Miss B.Lamade (GER) & Miss P.Schnyder (SUI) ....
16. **Miss E.S.H.Callens** (BEL) **& Miss M.Shaughnessy** (USA) **[6]**
Miss B.Lamade & Miss P.Schnyder 6/4 3/6 12/10

Miss I.Majoli & Miss H.Nagyova 6/2 6/4

Miss L.M.Raymond & Miss R.P.Stubbs [1] 6/3 6/2

17. **Miss S.Williams** (USA) **& Miss V.Williams** (USA) .....[4]
18. Miss M.E.Salerni (ARG) & Miss P.Tarabini (ARG) ....
Miss S.Williams & Miss V.Williams [4] 6/1 6/1
(W) 19. Miss J.Hopkins (USA) & Miss L.Latimer (GBR) ....
20. Miss N.Dechy (FRA) & Miss A.Mauresmo (FRA) ....
Miss N.Dechy & Miss A.Mauresmo 3/6 6/1 6/2

Miss S.Williams & Miss V.Williams [4] 6/3 6/3

Miss M.Navratilova & Miss A.Sanchez Vicario [16] ......w/o.

21. Miss Y.Basuki (INA) & Miss N.Miyagi (JPN) ....
22. Miss J.M.Pullin (GBR) & Miss L.A.Woodroffe (GBR) .....
Miss Y.Basuki & Miss N.Miyagi ......7/6(5) 2/6 6/2
23. Miss G.Casoni (ITA) & Miss S.Nacuk (YUG) ....
24. **Miss M.Navratilova** (USA) **& Miss A.Sanchez Vicario** (ESP) **[16]**
Miss M.Navratilova & Miss A.Sanchez Vicario [16] 6/0 6/1

Miss M.Navratilova & Miss A.Sanchez Vicario [16] 7/5 6/1

Mrs K.Po-Messerli & Miss N.Tauziat [5] 4/6 6/4 6/3

25. **Miss A.Fusai** (FRA) **& Miss R.Grande** (ITA) ....[10]
(W) 26. Miss H.Crook (GBR) & Miss V.E.Davies (GBR) ....
Miss A.Fusai & Miss R.Grande [10] 6/2 6/2
27. Miss M.J.Martinez (ESP) & Miss A.I.Medina Garrigues (ESP) ...
28. Miss N.Petrova (RUS) & Miss T.Pisnik (SLO) ....
Miss N.Petrova & Miss T.Pisnik 5/7 6/3 8/6

Miss N.Petrova & Miss T.Pisnik 4/6 6/4 6/4

Mrs K.Po-Messerli & Miss N.Tauziat [5] 6/3 6/3

29. Miss A.Jidkova (RUS) & Miss M.Tu (USA) ....
30. Miss C.Dhenin (FRA) & Miss M.Diaz-Oliva (ARG) ....
Miss C.Dhenin & Miss M.Diaz-Oliva ......6/3 7/6(3)
31. Miss T.Musgrave (AUS) & Miss I.Selyutina (KAZ) ....
32. **Mrs K.Po-Messerli** (USA) **& Miss N.Tauziat** (FRA) ....[5]
Mrs K.Po-Messerli & Miss N.Tauziat [5] 6/2 7/5

Mrs K.Po-Messerli & Miss N.Tauziat [5] 6/3 6/1

Miss L.M.Raymond & Miss R.P.Stubbs [1] 6/4 6/3

33. **Miss J.Dokic** (YUG) **& Miss C.Martinez** (ESP) ....[7]
34. Mrs R.Dragomir Ilie (ROM) & Miss A.Glass (GER) ....
Miss J.Dokic & Miss C.Martinez [7] 4/6 6/0 6/0
35. Miss E.Loit (FRA) & Miss A-G.Sidot (FRA) ....
(W) 36. Miss L.A.Ahl (GBR) & Miss H.Collin (GBR) ....
Miss E.Loit & Miss A-G.Sidot 6/3 6/2

Miss J.Dokic & Miss C.Martinez [7] ......6/4 6/7(5) 6/4

Miss K.Clijsters & Miss A.Sugiyama [9] 6/2 5/7 6/3

37. Miss V.Razzano (FRA) & Miss S.Testud (FRA) ....
38. Miss K.Grant (RSA) & Miss M.Weingartner (GER) ....
Miss V.Razzano & Miss S.Testud 6/1 6/3
39. Miss J.Lee (TPE) & Miss W.Prakusya (INA) ....
40. **Miss K.Clijsters** (BEL) **& Miss A.Sugiyama** (JPN) ....[9]
Miss K.Clijsters & Miss A.Sugiyama [9] 6/4 6/3

Miss K.Clijsters & Miss A.Sugiyama [9] ......6/3 7/6(4)

Miss K.Clijsters & Miss A.Sugiyama [9] 6/2 6/2

41. **Miss T.Krizan** (SLO) **& Miss K.Srebotnik** (SLO) ....[15]
42. Miss A.Bachmann (GER) & Miss B.Schwartz (AUT) ....
Miss T.Krizan & Miss K.Srebotnik [15] 6/2 6/4
43. Miss K.Habsudova (SVK) & Miss D.Hantuchova (SVK) .
44. Miss L.Bacheva (BUL) & Miss C.Torrens-Valero (ESP) ...
Miss K.Habsudova & Miss D.Hantuchova 6/3 4/6 6/1

Miss K.Habsudova & Miss D.Hantuchova 6/4 3/6 6/3

Miss R.McQuillan & Miss L.McShea 7/5 6/4

45. Miss R.McQuillan (AUS) & Miss L.McShea (AUS) ....
46. Miss R.Kolbovic (CAN) & Miss L.Osterloh (USA) ....
Miss R.McQuillan & Miss L.McShea ......6/2 7/6(5)
47. Miss E.Dyrberg (DEN) & Mrs K.Marosi-Aracama (HUN) .
48. **Miss C.Black** (ZIM) **& Miss E.Likhovtseva** (RUS) ....[3]
Miss C.Black & Miss E.Likhovtseva [3] 6/4 6/2

Miss R.McQuillan & Miss L.McShea 6/3 6/4

Miss K.Clijsters & Miss A.Sugiyama [9] 6/4 6/4

49. **Miss N.Arendt** (USA) **& Miss C.M.Vis** (NED) ....[8]
(Q) 50. Miss E.Martincova (CZE) & Miss T.Perebiynis (UKR) .....
Miss N.Arendt & Miss C.M.Vis [8] 6/3 6/4
51. Miss K-A.Guse (AUS) & Miss A.Molik (AUS) ....
(Q) 52. Miss M.Matevzic (SLO) & Miss D.Zaric (YUG) ....
Miss M.Matevzic & Miss D.Zaric ......6/7(2) 7/6(3) 6/4

Miss M.Matevzic & Miss D.Zaric 6/3 4/6 6/3

Miss M.Matevzic & Miss D.Zaric ......w/o.

53. Miss A.Carlsson (SWE) & Miss M.Maleeva (BUL) ....
54. Miss J.Henin (BEL) & Miss M.Serna (ESP) ....
Miss J.Henin & Miss M.Serna 5/7 7/5 6/3
55. Miss K.Boogert (NED) & Miss M.Oremans (NED) ....
56. **Miss N.J.Pratt** (AUS) **& Miss E.Tatarkova** (UKR) .....[11]
Miss K.Boogert & Miss M.Oremans 7/5 6/4

Miss J.Henin & Miss M.Serna 6/2 6/4

Miss V.Ruano Pascual & Miss P.Suarez [2] 6/3 3/6 6/1

57. **Miss A.Huber** (GER) **& Miss B.Schett** (AUT) ....[13]
58. Miss B.Rittner (GER) & Miss M.A.Vento (VEN) ....
Miss B.Rittner & Miss M.A.Vento 6/4 6/4
59. Miss E.Gagliardi (SUI) & Miss L.Golarsa (ITA) ....
(Q) 60. Miss D.Buth (USA) & Miss N.Grandin (RSA) ....
Miss D.Buth & Miss N.Grandin ......7/6(2) 6/7(4) 6/2

Miss B.Rittner & Miss M.A.Vento 6/1 6/1

Miss V.Ruano Pascual & Miss P.Suarez [2] 6/3 3/6 6/1

61. Miss A.Frazier (USA) & Miss K.Schlukebir (USA) ....
62. Mrs L.Huber (RSA) & Miss L.Montalvo (ARG) ....
Miss A.Frazier & Miss K.Schlukebir 6/3 6/4
63. Miss S.Plischke (AUT) & Miss V.Webb (CAN) ....
64. **Miss V.Ruano Pascual** (ESP) **& Miss P.Suarez** (ARG) .[2]
Miss V.Ruano Pascual & Miss P.Suarez [2] 6/3 6/0

Miss V.Ruano Pascual & Miss P.Suarez [2] 7/5 6/4

Miss K.Clijsters & Miss A.Sugiyama [9] 6/4 6/4

Miss L.M.Raymond & Miss R.P.Stubbs [1] 6/3 7/5

Miss L.M.Raymond & Miss R.P.Stubbs [1] 6/4 6/3

Miss V.Ruano Pascual & Miss P.Suarez [2]

Heavy type denotes seeded players. The figure in brackets against names denotes the order in which they have been seeded. (W) = Wild card. (Q) = Qualifier. (L) = Lucky loser.

The matches are the best of three sets

The winners become the holders, for the year only, of the CHALLENGE CUPS presented by the family of the late Mr S. H. SMITH and The All England Lawn Tennis and Croquet Club. The winners receive silver replicas of the Challenge Cup. A silver salver is presented to each of the runners-up and a bronze medal to each defeated semi-finalist.

First Round	Second Round	Third Round	Quarter-Finals	Semi-Finals	Final
1. **T.A.Woodbridge** (AUS) & **Miss R.P.Stubbs** (AUS) ....[1]					
2. P.Albano (ARG) & Miss A.Fusai (FRA)	T.A.Woodbridge & Miss R.P.Stubbs [1]				
3. L.Friedl (CZE) & Miss D.Hantuchova (SVK)	....6/3 6/2	L.Friedl &			
4. D.Bowen (USA) & Miss M.J.Martinez (ESP)	L.Friedl & Miss D.Hantuchova	Miss D.Hantuchova			
(W) 5. J.Davidson (GBR) & Miss V.E.Davies (GBR)	....6/0 6/3	....................................1/6 6/3 6/4	L.Friedl &		
6. J.Boutter (FRA) & Miss N.Dechy (FRA)	J.Boutter & Miss N.Dechy		Miss D.Hantuchova		
(W) 7. B.Cowan (GBR) & Miss J.M.Pullin (GBR)	....6/2 6/7(8) 6/4	J.Novak &	....................................7/6(2) 6/4		
8. **J.Novak** (CZE) & **Miss M.Oremans** (NED) ....[13]	J.Novak & Miss M.Oremans [13]	Miss M.Oremans [13]			
9. **R.Leach** (USA) & **Miss A.J.Coetzer** (RSA) ....[12]	....7/6(5) 6/4	.............................6/2 5/7 7/5		L.Friedl & Miss D.Hantuchova	
10. T.Shimada (JPN) & Miss N.Miyagi (JPN)	R.Leach & Miss A.J.Coetzer [12]			6/2 6/3	
11. B.MacPhie (USA) & Miss N.J.Pratt (AUS)	....7/5 6/7(4) 6/2	R.Leach &			
12. D.Adams (RSA) & Miss M.E.Salerni (ARG)	B.MacPhie & Miss N.J.Pratt	Miss A.J.Coetzer [12]			
13. D.Macpherson (AUS) & Miss R.McQuillan (AUS)	....7/6(1) 7/5	....................................7/6(3) 6/4	D.Johnson &		
14. T.Carbonell (ESP) & Miss V.Ruano Pascual (ESP)	T.Carbonell & Miss V.Ruano Pascual		Mrs K.Po-Messerli [5]		
(W)15. J.Nelson (GBR) & Miss H.Crook (GBR)	....6/2 4/6 6/4	D.Johnson &	....................................6/4 6/2		
16. **D.Johnson** (USA) & **Mrs K.Po-Messerli** (USA) ....[5]	D.Johnson & Mrs K.Po-Messerli [5]	Mrs K.Po-Messerli [5]			
17. **S.Stolle** (AUS) & **Miss C.Black** (ZIM) ....[3]	....6/0 6/3	.............................6/3 6/2			
18. S.Aspelin (SWE) & Miss T.Krizan (SLO)	S.Stolle & Miss C.Black [3]				
19. M.Damm (CZE) & Miss H.Nagyova (SVK)	....6/3 6/4	M.Damm &			
20. A.Portas (ESP) & Miss A.I.Medina Garrigues (ESP)	M.Damm & Miss H.Nagyova	Miss H.Nagyova			
21. A.Schneiter (ITA) & Miss R.Hiraki (JPN)	....7/6(8) 7/5	....................................6/4 6/4	D.Rikl &		
22. L.Manta (SUI) & Miss L.Golarsa (ITA)	L.Manta & Miss L.Golarsa		Miss K.Habsudova [15]		
23. A.Olhovskiy (RUS) & Miss S.Plischke (AUT)	....6/3 6/4	D.Rikl &	....................................6/3 6/2		
24. **D.Rikl** (CZE) & **Miss K.Habsudova** (SVK) ....[15]	D.Rikl & Miss K.Habsudova [15]	Miss K.Habsudova [15]			
25. **M.Knowles** (BAH) & **Miss N.Arendt** (USA) ....[9]	....6/4 7/6(6) 0/0	.............................6/4 6/4		D.Rikl & Miss K.Habsudova [15]	
(W)26. S.Capriati (USA) & Miss J.Capriati (USA)	M.Knowles & Miss N.Arendt [9]			6/3 6/2	
27. C.Suk (CZE) & Miss M.Shaughnessy (USA)	....6/1 6/4	M.Knowles &			
28. G.Stafford (RSA) & Miss L.M.McNeil (USA)	G.Stafford & Miss L.M.McNeil	Miss N.Arendt [9]			
29. M.Hill (AUS) & Miss K.Boogert (NED)	....6/3 6/4	....................................7/5 3/6 6/4	M.Wakefield &		
30. M.Wakefield (RSA) & Miss N.De Villiers (RSA)	M.Wakefield & Miss N.De Villiers		Miss N.De Villiers		
31. J-L.De Jager (RSA) & E.Tatarkova (UKR)	....4/6 6/3 11/9	M.Wakefield &	....................................6/4 4/6 7/5		
32. **J.Palmer** (USA) & **Miss A.Sanchez Vicario** (ESP) ....[7]	J-L.De Jager & Miss E.Tatarkova	Miss N.De Villiers			
33. **L.Paes** (IND) & **Miss L.M.Raymond** (USA) ....[6]	....6/4 6/4	.............................6/2 6/2			
34. M.Barnard (RSA) & Miss C.M.Vis (NED)	L.Paes & Miss L.M.Raymond [6]				
35. M.Mirnyi (BLR) & Miss M.Navratilova (USA)	....6/2 6/1	L.Paes &			
36. M.Sprengelmeyer (USA) & Miss L.Osterloh (USA)	M.Mirnyi & Miss M.Navratilova	Miss L.M.Raymond [6]			
37. B.Bryan (USA) & Miss L.McShea (AUS)	....6/4 7/5	....................................6/3 6/4	B.Bryan &		
38. J.Thomas (USA) & Miss J.Lee (TPE)	B.Bryan & Miss L.McShea		Miss L.McShea		
39. A.Fisher (AUS) & Miss K.Grant (RSA)	....6/2 7/5	B.Bryan &	....................................5/7 7/5 7/5		
40. **P.Pala** (CZE) & **Miss J.Husarova** (SVK) ....[11]	A.Fisher & Miss K.Grant	Miss L.McShea			
41. **J.Tarango** (USA) & **Miss J.Dokic** (YUG) ....[14]	....1/6 6/2 6/4	.............................6/4 6/4		M.Bhupathi & Miss E.Likhovtseva [4]	
42. J.Coetzee (RSA) & Miss C.Rubin (USA)	J.Tarango & Miss J.Dokic [14]			6/1 4/6 15/13	
43. R.Koenig (RSA) & Miss A.Ellwood (AUS)	....3/6 6/4 6/1	J.Tarango &			
44. C.Haggard (RSA) & Miss E.S.H.Callens (BEL)	C.Haggard & Miss E.S.H.Callens	Miss J.Dokic [14]			
45. A.Florent (AUS) & Miss A.Huber (GER)	....6/7(7) 6/3 6/4	....................................w./o.	M.Bhupathi &		
46. A.Kratzmann (AUS) & Miss M.Serna (ESP)	A.Kratzmann & Miss M.Serna		Miss E.Likhovtseva [4]		
47. S.Humphries (USA) & Miss A-G.Sidot (FRA)	....7/6(2) 2/6 6/2	M.Bhupathi &	....................................6/4 4/6 6/4		
48. **M.Bhupathi** (IND) & **Miss E.Likhovtseva** (RUS) ....[4]	M.Bhupathi & Miss E.Likhovtseva [4]	Miss E.Likhovtseva [4]			
49. **J.Eagle** (AUS) & **Miss B.Schett** (AUT) ....[8]	....6/4 6/4	.............................6/4 4/6 6/2			
50. J.Weir Smith (RSA) & Miss K.Schlukebir (USA)	J.Weir Smith & Miss K.Schlukebir				
51. K.Braasch (GER) & Miss B.Rittner (GER)	....6/4 7/5	K.Braasch &			
52. P.Hanley (AUS) & Miss S.Jeyaseelan (CAN)	K.Braasch & Miss B.Rittner	Miss B.Rittner			
53. J.Landsberg (SWE) & A.Carlsson (SWE)	....3/6 7/6(4) 6/4	....................................6/1 6/4	M.Bryan &		
54. M.Bryan (USA) & Mrs L.Huber (RSA)	M.Bryan & Mrs L.Huber		Mrs L.Huber		
55. J.Waite (USA) & Miss K-A.Guse (AUS)	....6/7(5) 6/3 9/7	M.Bryan &	....................................7/6(2) 3/6 13/11		
56. **L.Arnold** (ARG) & **Miss P.Suarez** (ARG) ....[10]	L.Arnold & Miss P.Suarez [10]	Mrs L.Huber			
57. **P.Vizner** (CZE) & **Miss T.Garbin** (ITA) ....[16]	....6/3 7/5	.............................6/4 6/2		M.Bryan & Mrs L.Huber	
58. M.Hood (ARG) & Miss T.Poutchek (BLR)	P.Vizner & Miss T.Garbin [16]			6/3 6/2	
(W)59. K.Spencer (GBR) & Miss L.A.Woodroffe (GBR)	....5/7 6/3 6/4	T.Vanhoudt &			
60. T.Vanhoudt (BEL) & Miss K.Srebotnik (SLO)	T.Vanhoudt & Miss K.Srebotnik	Miss K.Srebotnik			
61. D.Nargiso (ITA) & Miss I.Tulyaganova (UZB)	....7/6(5) 6/3	....................................6/3 3/6 6/0	E.Ferreira &		
62. M.Garcia (ARG) & Miss L.Montalvo (ARG)	M.Garcia & Miss L.Montalvo		Miss A.Sugiyama [2]		
63. B.Haygarth (RSA) & Miss P.Tarabini (ARG)	....6/4 7/6(4)	E.Ferreira &	....................................6/3 2/6 9/7		
64. **E.Ferreira** (RSA) & **Miss A.Sugiyama** (JPN) ....[2]	E.Ferreira & Miss A.Sugiyama [2]	Miss A.Sugiyama [2]			
	....6/4 6/3	.............................7/5 6/1			

Final:

L.Friedl & Miss D.Hantuchova 4/6 6/3 6/2

Semi-finals path:

L.Friedl & Miss D.Hantuchova 6/2 5/7 7/3

M.Bryan & Mrs L.Huber 6/2 6/2

Heavy type denotes seeded players. The figure in brackets against names denotes the order in which they have been seeded. (W) = Wild card. (Q) = Qualifier. (L) = Lucky loser.

The matches are the best of three sets

THE 35 AND OVER GENTLEMEN'S INVITATION DOUBLES

The winners become the holders, for the year only, of a Cup presented by The All England Lawn Tennis and Croquet Club. The winners receive miniature silver salvers. A silver medal is presented to each of the runners-up.

Holders: K. Flach and R. Seguso and M. J. Bates and N. A. Fulwood (shared)

GROUP A

GROUP A	M.J.Bates (GBR) and N.A.Fulwood (GBR)	P.Aldrich (RSA) and D.Visser (RSA)	J.Grabb (USA) and J.Pugh (USA)	P.Hand (GBR) and R.Krishnan (IND)	WINS	LOSSES
M.J.Bates (GBR) and N.A.Fulwood (GBR)		7/5 6/4 W	6/2 6/7(8) 4/6 L	6/4 4/6 6/4 W	2	1
P.Aldrich (RSA) and D.Visser (RSA)	5/7 4/6 L		5/7 7/6(1) 4/6 L	1/6 6/7(5) L	0	3
J.Grabb (USA) and J.Pugh (USA)	2/6 7/6(8) 6/4 W	7/5 6/7(1) 6/4 W		7/5 6/7(4) 9/7 W	3	0
P.Hand (GBR) and R.Krishnan (IND)	4/6 6/4 4/6 L	6/1 7/6(5) W	5/7 7/6(4) 7/9 L		1	2

GROUP B

GROUP B	J.B.Fitzgerald (AUS) and W.Masur (AUS)	H.Guenthardt (SUI) and B.Taroczy (HUN)	D.Cahill (AUS) and C.J.Van Rensburg (RSA)	C.Panatta (ITA) and D.Rostagno (USA)	WINS	LOSSES
J.B.Fitzgerald (AUS) and W.Masur (AUS)		6/1 6/2 W	5/7 6/4 13/11 W	6/2 6/4 W	3	0
H.Guenthardt (SUI) and B.Taroczy (HUN)	1/6 2/6 L		W/O	4/6 1/6 L	0	3
D.Cahill (AUS) and C.J.Van Rensburg (RSA)	7/5 4/6 11/13 L	W/O W		2/6 7/6(2) 15/13 W	2	1
C.Panatta (ITA) and D.Rostagno (USA)	2/6 4/6 L	6/4 6/1 W	6/2 6/7(2) 13/15 L		1	2

GROUP C

GROUP C	A.Jarryd (SWE) and J.Nystrom (SWE)	L.Shiras (USA) and T.Wilkison (USA)	G.W.Donnelly (USA) and L.Jensen (USA)	J.Hlasek (SUI) and S.Zivojinovic (YUG)	WINS	LOSSES
A.Jarryd (SWE) and J.Nystrom (SWE)		6/2 7/5 W	6/7(4) 3/6 L	6/3 7/6(4) W	2	1
L.Shiras (USA) and T.Wilkison (USA)	2/6 5/7 L		6/4 3/6 6/3 W	6/4 6/3 W	2	1
G.W.Donnelly (USA) and L.Jensen (USA)	7/6(4) 6/3 W	4/6 6/3 3/6 L		3/6 6/3 4/6 L	1	2
J.Hlasek (SUI) and S.Zivojinovic (YUG)	3/6 6/7(4) L	4/6 3/6 L	6/3 3/6 6/4 W		1	2

GROUP D

GROUP D	K.Curren (USA) and J.Kriek (USA)	S.Casal (ESP) and E.Sanchez (ESP)	M.Bahrami (IRI) and H.Leconte (FRA)	S.Davis (USA) and D.Pate (USA)	WINS	LOSSES
K.Curren (USA) and J.Kriek (USA)		7/6(10) 6/4 W	5/7 6/1 3/6 L	6/7(5) 6/3 4/6 L	1	2
S.Casal (ESP) and E.Sanchez (ESP)	6/7(10) 4/6 L		7/5 4/6 6/3 W	7/6(9) 7/6(5) W	2	1
M.Bahrami (IRI) and H.Leconte (FRA)	7/5 1/6 6/3 W	5/7 6/4 3/6 L		3/6 1/6 L	1	2
S.Davis (USA) and D.Pate (USA)	7/6(5) 3/6 6/4 W	6/7(9) 6/7(5) L	6/3 6/1 W		2	1

SEMI-FINAL

J.Grabb (USA) and J.Pugh (USA) / J.B.Fitzgerald (AUS) and W.Masur (AUS) — 5/7 6/3 11/9

A.Jarryd (SWE) and J.Nystrom (SWE) / S.Casal (ESP) and E.Sanchez (ESP) — 7/6(3) 6/4

FINAL

J.B.Fitzgerald (AUS) and W.Masur (AUS) — 7/6(2) 6/0

This event is played on a 'round robin' basis. Sixteen invited pairs are divided into four groups and each pair in each group plays the others. The pairs winning most matches are the winners of their respective groups and play semi-final and final rounds as indicated above. If matches should be equal in any group, the head-to-head result between the two pairs with the same number of wins determines the winning pair of the group. Heavy type denotes seeded players. **The matches are the best of three sets.** The tie-break operates at six games all in the first two sets.

THE 45 AND OVER GENTLEMEN'S INVITATION DOUBLES

The winners become the holders, for the year only, of a Cup presented by The All England Lawn Tennis and Croquet Club. The winners receive miniature silver salvers. A silver medal is presented to each of the runners-up.

Holders: P. Fleming and A. A. Mayer

Heavy type denotes seeded players. The figure in brackets against names denotes the order in which they have been seeded. **The matches are the best of three sets.** The tie-break operates at six games all in the first two sets.

First Round

1. P.Fleming (USA) & A.A.Mayer (USA) ....[1]
2. bye
3. M.C.Riessen & S.E.Stewart (USA)
4. J.Kodes (CZE) & M.Santana (ESP)
5. bye
6. I.Nastase (ROM) & T.S.Okker (NED)
7. bye
8. J.W.Feaver (GBR) & J.M.Lloyd (GBR)
9. B.E.Gottfried (USA) & T.R.Gullikson (USA) ....[3]
10. bye
11. P.Slozil (CZE) & T.Smid (CZE)
12. bye
13. J.D.Newcombe (AUS) & A.D.Roche (AUS)
14. bye
15. C.Dowdeswell (GBR) & C.J.Mottram (GBR)
16. O.K.Davidson (AUS) & F.S.Stolle (AUS)
17. bye
18. J.G.Alexander (AUS) & P.Dent (AUS)
19. R.L.Stockton (USA) & R.Tanner (USA)
20. bye
21. M.R.Edmondson (AUS) & R.J.Frawley (AUS)
22. H.Pfister (USA) & D.Ralston (USA)
23. bye
24. A.Amritraj (IND) & V.Amritraj (IND) ....[4]
25. R.Drysdale (GBR) & G.Mayer (USA)
26. bye
27. R.L.Case (AUS) & G.Masters (AUS)
28. bye
29. E.C.Drysdale (RSA) & R.A.J.Hewitt (RSA)
30. R.C.Lutz (USA) & S.R.Smith (USA)
31. bye
32. P.B.McNamara (AUS) & P.F.McNamee (AUS) ......[2]

Second Round

- P.Fleming & A.A.Mayer [1]
- M.C.Riessen & S.E.Stewart ......7/6(4) 7/6(2)
- I.Nastase & T.S.Okker
- J.W.Feaver & J.M.Lloyd
- B.E.Gottfried & T.R.Gullikson [3]
- P.Slozil & T.Smid
- J.D.Newcombe & A.D.Roche
- C.Dowdeswell & C.J.Mottram 6/2 6/2
- J.G.Alexander & P.Dent
- R.L.Stockton & R.Tanner
- M.R.Edmondson & R.J.Frawley 6/4 6/4
- A.Amritraj & V.Amritraj [4]
- R.Drysdale & G.Mayer
- R.L.Case & G.Masters
- R.C.Lutz & S.R.Smith 4/6 6/3 6/2
- P.B.McNamara & P.F.McNamee [2]

Quarter-Finals

- P.Fleming & A.A.Mayer [1] 6/2 6/3
- J.W.Feaver & J.M.Lloyd 6/2 6/2
- B.E.Gottfried & T.R.Gullikson [3] ......7/6(2) 7/6(9)
- C.Dowdeswell & C.J.Mottram 6/3 6/3
- J.G.Alexander & P.Dent 7/5 7/5
- M.R.Edmondson & R.J.Frawley ......6/7(2) 6/4 11/9
- R.Drysdale & G.Mayer ......7/6(4) 4/6 3/2 Ret'd
- P.B.McNamara & P.F.McNamee [2] 6/2 6/2

Semi-Finals

- P.Fleming & A.A.Mayer [1] 4/6 6/1 6/1
- C.Dowdeswell & C.J.Mottram ......7/6(3) 6/3
- J.G.Alexander & P.Dent ......7/6(6) 7/5
- P.B.McNamara & P.F.McNamee [2] ......6/4 6/7(2) 6/2

Final

- C.Dowdeswell & C.J.Mottram ......6/4 7/6(4)
- P.B.McNamara & P.F.McNamee [2] 6/4 6/3

THE 35 AND OVER LADIES' INVITATION DOUBLES

Holders: Mrs R. Nideffer and Miss Y. Vermaak

GROUP A	Miss H.Sukova (CZE) and Miss Y.Vermaak (RSA)	Miss J.M.Durie (GBR) and Miss M.Jausovec (SLO)	Mrs G.Magers (USA) and Miss W.M.Turnbull (AUS)	Miss R.Casals (USA) and Miss S.Collins (USA)	WINS	LOSSES	FINAL
Miss H.Sukova (CZE) and Miss Y.Vermaak (RSA)		6/4 6/7(3) 4/6 L	1/6 6/3 3/6 L	5/7 6/4 6/1 W	1	2	
Miss J.M.Durie (GBR) and Miss M.Jausovec (SLO)	4/6 7/6(3) 6/4 W		7/5 2/6 6/4 W	6/2 6/1 W	3	0	
Mrs G.Magers (USA) and Miss W.M.Turnbull (AUS)	6/1 3/6 6/3 W	5/7 6/2 4/6 L		7/5 7/5 W	2	1	
Miss R.Casals (USA) and Miss S.Collins (USA)	7/5 4/6 1/6 L	2/6 1/6 L	5/7 5/7 L		0	3	

GROUP B	Miss P.Shriver (USA) and Miss S.V.Wade (GBR)	Miss K.Lindqvist (SWE) and Miss G.R.Stevens (RSA)	Miss I.Kloss (RSA) and Mrs R.Nideffer (RSA)	Miss J.Hetherington (USA) and Miss J.C.Russell (USA)	WINS	LOSSES	FINAL
Miss P.Shriver (USA) and Miss S.V.Wade (GBR)		3/6 5/7 L	0/6 0/6 L	2/6 2/6 L	0	3	
Miss K.Lindqvist (SWE) and Miss G.R.Stevens (RSA)	6/3 7/5 W		7/5 5/7 4/6 L	2/6 2/6 L	1	2	
Miss I.Kloss (RSA) and Mrs R.Nideffer (RSA)	6/0 6/0 W	5/7 7/5 6/4 W		6/4 6/4 W	3	0	
Miss J.Hetherington (USA) and Miss J.C.Russell (USA)	6/2 6/2 W	6/2 6/2 W	4/6 4/6 L		2	1	

RESULTS

FINAL:
Miss J.M.Durie (GBR) and Miss M.Jausovec (SLO)

Miss I.Kloss (RSA) and Mrs R.Nideffer (RSA)

Miss I.Kloss (RSA) and Mrs R.Nideffer (RSA) 6/4 5/7 6/3

This event is played on a 'round robin' basis. Eight invited pairs are divided into two groups and each pair in each group plays the others. The pairs winning most matches are the winners of their respective groups and play a final round as indicated above. If matches should be equal in any group, the head-to-head result between the two pairs with the same number of wins determines the winning pair of the group.

Heavy type denotes seeded players.

The matches are the best of three sets. The tie-break operates at six games all in the first two sets.

ALPHABETICAL LIST — 35 AND OVER EVENTS

GENTLEMEN

Aldrich P. *(South Africa)*
Bahrami M. *(Iran)*
Bates M.J. *(Great Britain)*
Cahill D. *(Australia)*
Casal S. *(Spain)*
Curren K. *(USA)*
Davis S. *(USA)*
Donnelly G.W. *(USA)*

Fitzgerald J.B. *(Australia)*
Fulwood N.A. *(Great Britain)*
Grabb J. *(USA)*
Guenthardt H. *(Switzerland)*
Hand P. *(Great Britain)*
Hlasek J. *(Switzerland)*
Jarryd A. *(Sweden)*
Jensen L. *(USA)*

Kriek J. *(USA)*
Krishnan R. *(India)*
Leconte H. *(France)*
Masur W. *(Australia)*
Nystrom J. *(Sweden)*
Panatta C. *(Italy)*
Pate D. *(USA)*
Pugh J. *(USA)*

Rostagno D. *(USA)*
Sanchez E. *(Spain)*
Shiras L. *(USA)*
Taroczy B. *(Hungary)*
Van Rensburg C.J. *(South Africa)*
Visser D. *(South Africa)*
Wilkison T. *(USA)*
Zivojinovic S. *(Yugoslavia)*

LADIES

Casals Miss R. *(USA)*
Collins Miss S. *(USA)*
Durie Miss J.M. *(Great Britain)*
Hetherington Miss J. *(USA)*

Jausovec Miss M. *(Slovenia)*
Kloss Miss I. *(South Africa)*
Lindqvist Miss C. *(Sweden)*
Magers Mrs G. *(USA)*

Nideffer Mrs R. *(South Africa)*
Russell Miss J.C. *(USA)*
Shriver Miss P. *(USA)*
Stevens Miss G.R. *(South Africa)*

Sukova Miss H. *(Czech Republic)*
Turnbull Miss W.M. *(Australia)*
Vermaak Miss Y. *(South Africa)*
Wade Miss S.V. *(Great Britain)*

ALPHABETICAL LIST — 45 AND OVER EVENT

GENTLEMEN

Alexander J.G. *(Australia)*
Amritraj A. *(India)*
Amritraj V. *(India)*
Case R.L. *(Australia)*
Davidson O.K. *(Australia)*
Dent P. *(Australia)*
Dowdeswell C. *(Great Britain)*
Drysdale E.C. *(South Africa)*
Drysdale R. *(Great Britain)*
Edmondson M.R. *(Australia)*

Feaver J.W. *(Great Britain)*
Fleming P. *(USA)*
Frawley R.J. *(Australia)*
Gottfried B.E. *(USA)*
Gullikson T.R. *(USA)*
Hewitt R.A.J. *(South Africa)*
Kodes J. *(Czech Republic)*
Lloyd J.M. *(Great Britain)*
Lutz R.C. *(USA)*
Masters G. *(Australia)*

Mayer G. *(USA)*
Mayer A.A. *(USA)*
McNamara P.B. *(Australia)*
McNamee P.F. *(Australia)*
Mottram C.J. *(Great Britain)*
Nastase I. *(Romania)*
Newcombe J.D. *(Australia)*
Okker T.S. *(Netherlands)*
Pfister H. *(USA)*
Ralston D. *(USA)*

Riessen M.C. *(USA)*
Roche A.D. *(Australia)*
Santana M. *(Spain)*
Slozil P. *(Czech Republic)*
Smid T. *(Czech Republic)*
Smith S.R. *(USA)*
Stewart S.E. *(USA)*
Stockton R.L. *(USA)*
Stolle F.S. *(Australia)*
Tanner R. *(USA)*

THE BOYS' SINGLES CHAMPIONSHIP

Holder: N. Mahut

For both the Boys' Singles *and* the Boys' Doubles Championships, the winners become the holders, for the year only, of a cup presented by The All England Lawn Tennis and Croquet Club. The winners each receive a miniature Cup and the runners-up receive mementoes.

First Round		Second Round	Third Round	Quarter-Finals	Semi-Finals	Final

First Round:
1. **J.Tipsarevic [1]** ....(YUG)
2. (W) T.Pocock ....(GBR)
3. (Q) P.Amritraj ....(USA)
4. (Q) B.Baker ....(USA)
5. S.Tuksar ....(CRO)
6. M.Zgaga ....(SLO)
7. S.Wiespeiner ....(AUT)
8. **T.Reid [16]** ....(AUS)
9. **L.Vitullo [12]** ....(ARG)
10. S.Stadler ....(GER)
11. M.Emery ....(USA)
12. A.Banks ....(GBR)
13. C.Johansson ....(SWE)
14. D.Brewer ....(GBR)
15. (Q) R.Durek ....(AUS)
16. **Y-T.Wang [6]** ....(TPE)
17. **B.Echagaray [3]** ....(MEX)
18. A.Brizzi ....(ITA)
19. B.Gronefeld ....(GER)
20. (W) R.Hutchins ....(GBR)
21. F.Dancevic ....(CAN)
22. J.Masik ....(CZE)
23. F.Lemke ....(GER)
24. **P.Capdeville [15]** ....(CHI)
25. **R.Valent [10]** ....(SUI)
26. A.Cruciat ....(ROM)
27. B.Balleret ....(FRA)
28. M.Melo ....(BRA)
29. (W) M.Smith ....(GBR)
30. B.De Gier ....(NED)
31. R.Russell ....(JAM)
32. **Y.Abougzir [7]** ....(USA)
33. **F.Mayer [8]** ....(GER)
34. (W) N.Lalji ....(GBR)
35. (W) C.Evans ....(GBR)
36. (Q) S.Sipaeya ....(IND)
37. (Q) K.Skupski ....(GBR)
38. M.Egger ....(AUT)
39. (Q) I.Kanev ....(BUL)
40. **R.Soderling [9]** ....(SWE)
41. **S.Bohli [13]** ....(SUI)
42. (W) R.Bloomfield ....(GBR)
43. M.Auradou ....(FRA)
44. L.Gregorc ....(SLO)
45. (Q) P.Petzschner ....(GER)
46. J.Chu ....(USA)
47. M.Baghdatis ....(CYP)
48. **B.Dabul [4]** ....(ARG)
49. **A.Falla Ramirez [5]** ....(COL)
50. J.Cohen ....(USA)
51. S.Gonzalez ....(MEX)
52. A.Bogdanovic ....(GBR)
53. M.Bayer ....(GER)
54. C.Morel ....(FRA)
55. (W) G.Lapentti ....(ECU)
56. (W) L.Ouahab [11] ....(ALG)
57. **L.Noviski [14]** ....(ARG)
58. R.Henry ....(AUS)
59. C.Jacobs ....(RSA)
60. D.Kollerer ....(AUT)
61. D.Mihailovic ....(YUG)
62. (Q) H.Heyl ....(RSA)
63. O.Posada ....(VEN)
64. **G.Muller [2]** ....(LUX)

Second Round:
- J.Tipsarevic [1] 6/1 6/3
- B.Baker 4/6 6/3 6/4
- S.Tuksar ....6/7(5) 6/4 6/3
- T.Reid [16] ....6/3 7/6(5)
- L.Vitullo [12] 7/5 5/7 6/3
- M.Emery 5/7 7/5 6/4
- C.Johansson 6/3 6/4
- Y-T.Wang [6] ......7/5 6/7(7) 6/3
- A.Brizzi 6/3 2/6 6/2
- R.Hutchins 3/6 7/5 6/3
- F.Dancevic 6/4 6/3
- P.Capdeville [15] 6/0 6/1
- R.Valent [10] 7/5 6/3
- M.Melo 6/2 6/3
- M.Smith 7/5 6/1
- R.Russell ....1/6 7/6(9) 6/3
- F.Mayer [8] 6/2 7/5
- S.Sipaeya 6/4 6/4
- K.Skupski 6/3 6/3
- R.Soderling [9] 6/3 6/4
- S.Bohli [13] 6/4 6/4
- L.Gregorc ....6/2 7/6(2)
- P.Petzschner 3/6 6/3 6/1
- M.Baghdatis ....6/7(6) 7/5 9/7
- A.Falla Ramirez [5] 6/4 6/1
- S.Gonzalez 6/3 6/4
- M.Bayer 3/6 7/5 8/6
- G.Lapentti 6/2 6/1
- L.Noviski [14] 7/5 6/3
- C.Jacobs 6/1 6/4
- D.Mihailovic 6/3 7/5
- G.Muller [2] 4/6 6/4 11/9

Third Round:
- J.Tipsarevic [1] ......7/6(4) 3/6 6/3
- T.Reid [16] ....4/6 7/6(3) 7/5
- L.Vitullo [12] 6/0 6/4
- Y-T.Wang [6] 6/2 6/1
- A.Brizzi 6/4 4/6 10/8
- F.Dancevic 6/4 6/3
- R.Valent [10] 6/4 6/3
- R.Russell ....6/2 7/6(4)
- S.Sipaeya 7/5 7/5
- K.Skupski ....6/4 6/7(5) 6/3
- S.Bohli [13] 6/4 6/1
- P.Petzschner ....7/6(2) 6/4
- A.Falla Ramirez [5] 6/3 6/4
- G.Lapentti 6/3 6/4
- L.Noviski [14] 6/4 6/2
- G.Muller [2] 6/4 6/2

Quarter-Finals:
- T.Reid [16] 3/6 6/2 6/4
- Y-T.Wang [6] 6/3 6/2
- F.Dancevic 3/6 7/5 6/1
- R.Valent [10] 6/3 6/3
- K.Skupski 6/3 4/6 6/4
- P.Petzschner 6/2 6/4
- G.Lapentti ....6/1 6/7(5) 6/3
- G.Muller [2] 6/0 6/1

Semi-Finals:
- Y-T.Wang [6] 6/3 7/5
- R.Valent [10] ....7/6(6) 6/2
- P.Petzschner ...6/2 7/6(4)
- G.Muller [2] ....7/6(2) 7/6(5)

Final:
- R.Valent [10] 4/6 6/4 6/3
- G.Muller [2] ....6/3 7/6(3)

R.Valent [10] 3/6 7/5 6/3

THE BOYS' DOUBLES CHAMPIONSHIP

Holders: D. Coene and K. Vliegen

First Round:
1. **B.Echagaray (MEX) & S.Gonzalez (MEX)** ....[1]
2. J.Cohen (USA) & R.Durek (AUS) ....
3. J.Chu (USA) & M.Zgaga (SLO) ....
4. S.Bohli (SUI) & S.Tuksar (CRO) ....
5. C.Letcher (AUS) & S.Sipaeya (IND) ....
6. (W) R.Hutchins (GBR) & B.Riby (GBR) ....
7. R.Blair (RSA) & C.Jacobs (RSA) ....
8. **P.Capdeville (CHI) & O.Posada (VEN)** ....[7]
9. **T.Berdych (CZE) & B.De Gier (NED)** ....[3]
10. B.Baker (USA) & M.Emery (USA) ....
11. L.Gregorc (SLO) & R.Russell (JAM) ....
12. C.Johansson (SWE) & R.Soderling (SWE) ....
13. P.Amritraj (USA) & S.Amritraj (USA) ....
14. H.Heyl (RSA) & P.Ivanov (RUS) ....
15. L.Ouahab (ALG) & Y-T.Wang (TPE) ....
16. **M.Melo (BRA) & L.Noviski (ARG)** ....[5]
17. **R.Henry (AUS) & T.Reid (AUS)** ....[6]
18. P.Petzschner (GER) & S.Stadler (GER) ....
19. M.Bayer (GER) & F.Mayer (GER) ....
20. T.Gabashvili (RUS) & T.Pocock (GBR) ....
21. A.Chadaj (POL) & J.Masik (CZE) ....
22. H.Adjei-Darko (GHA) & K.Loglo (TGA) ....
23. R.Bloomfield (GBR) & J.Olsen (NZL) ....
24. **Y.Abougzir (USA) & L.Vitullo (ARG)** ....[4]
25. **F.Dancevic (CAN) & G.Lapentti (ECU)** ....[8]
26. (W) D.Brewer (GBR) & G.Thomas (GBR) ....
27. C.Evans (GBR) & M.Smith (GBR) ....
28. I.Kanev (BUL) & G.Kovacevic (AUS) ....
29. D.Kollerer (AUT) & S.Wiespeiner (AUT) ....
30. B.Balleret (FRA) & G.Muller (LUX) ....
31. A.Brizzi (ITA) & J.Zimmermann (USA) ....
32. **A.Falla Ramirez (COL) & C.Salamanca (COL)** .[2]

Second Round:
- B.Echagaray & S.Gonzalez [1] 6/1 6/3
- J.Chu & M.Zgaga 6/3 6/3
- C.Letcher & S.Sipaeya 6/0 6/3
- P.Capdeville & O.Posada [7] ......7/6(4) 1/6 6/2
- B.Baker & M.Emery ....6/3 6/7(7) 6/3
- L.Gregorc & R.Russell 6/4 4/6 6/3
- H.Heyl & P.Ivanov 7/5 6/3
- L.Ouahab & Y-T.Wang 6/3 1/6 8/6
- P.Petzschner & S.Stadler ....6/7(2) 6/4 6/1
- M.Bayer & F.Mayer ....6/4 7/6(5)
- A.Chadaj & J.Masik ....6/7(4) 7/6(6) 11/9
- R.Bloomfield & J.Olsen ....6/7(4) 6/2 6/4
- F.Dancevic & G.Lapentti [8] ....6/3 7/6(2)
- I.Kanev & G.Kovacevic 6/3 7/5
- B.Balleret & G.Muller ....4/6 7/6(2) 6/2
- A.Brizzi & J.Zimmermann ...6/7(12) 7/6(5) 6/4

Quarter-Finals:
- B.Echagaray & S.Gonzalez [1] ....6/4 7/6(4)
- C.Letcher & S.Sipaeya 6/2 6/4
- L.Gregorc & R.Russell 6/2 6/3
- H.Heyl & P.Ivanov 6/4 7/5
- P.Petzschner & S.Stadler 6/2 6/2
- A.Chadaj & J.Masik 6/3 6/4
- F.Dancevic & G.Lapentti [8] ....6/7(6) 6/4 6/4
- B.Balleret & G.Muller 5/7 6/3 10/8

Semi-Finals:
- B.Echagaray & S.Gonzalez [1] ....6/3 7/6(4)
- L.Gregorc & R.Russell 6/2 6/4
- P.Petzschner & S.Stadler 6/2 6/1
- F.Dancevic & G.Lapentti [8] 6/4 6/3

Final:
- B.Echagaray & S.Gonzalez [1] 4/6 7/6(3) 6/4
- F.Dancevic & G.Lapentti [8] 6/7(5) 6/2 6/4

F.Dancevic & G.Lapentti [8] 6/1 6/4

Heavy type denotes seeded players. The figure in brackets against names denotes the order in which they have been seeded. (W) = Wild card. (Q) = Qualifier. (L) = Lucky loser.

The matches are the best of three sets

THE GIRLS' SINGLES CHAMPIONSHIP

Holder: Miss M. E. Salerni

THE GIRLS' DOUBLES CHAMPIONSHIP

Holders: Miss I. Gaspar and Miss T. Perebiynis

Heavy type denotes seeded players. The figure in brackets against names denotes the order in which they have been seeded. (W) = Wild card. (Q) = Qualifier. (L) = Lucky loser.

The matches are the best of three sets

Year	Champion / Runner-up	Year	Champion / Runner-up	Year	Champion / Runner-up	Year	Champion / Runner-up	Year	Champion / Runner-up
1877	S. W. Gore / *W. C. Marshall*	1900	R. F. Doherty / *S. H. Smith*	1927	H. Cochet / *J. Borotra*	★ 1956	L. A. Hoad / *K. R. Rosewall*	1979	B. Borg / *R. Tanner*
1878	P. F. Hadow / *S. W. Gore*	1901	A. W. Gore / *R. F. Doherty*	1928	R. Lacoste / *H. Cochet*	1957	L. A. Hoad / *A. J. Cooper*	1980	B. Borg / *J. P. McEnroe*
★ 1879	J. T. Hartley / *V. St. L. Goold*	1902	H. L. Doherty / *A. W. Gore*	1929	H. Cochet / *J. Borotra*	★ 1958	A. J. Cooper / *N. A. Fraser*	1981	J. P. McEnroe / *B. Borg*
1880	J. T. Hartley / *H. F. Lawford*	1903	H. L. Doherty / *F. L. Riseley*	1930	W. T. Tilden / *W. Allison*	★ 1959	A. Olmedo / *R. Laver*	1982	J. S. Connors / *J. P. McEnroe*
1881	W. Renshaw / *J. T. Hartley*	1904	H. L. Doherty / *F. L. Riseley*	★ 1931	S. B. Wood / *F. X. Shields*	★ 1960	N. A. Fraser / *R. Laver*	1983	J. P. McEnroe / *C. J. Lewis*
1882	W. Renshaw / *E. Renshaw*	1905	H. L. Doherty / *N. E. Brookes*	1932	H. E. Vines / *H. W. Austin*	1961	R. Laver / *C. R. McKinley*	1984	J. P. McEnroe / *J. S. Connors*
1883	W. Renshaw / *E. Renshaw*	1906	H. L. Doherty / *F. L. Riseley*	1933	J. H. Crawford / *H. E. Vines*	1962	R. Laver / *M. F. Mulligan*	1985	B. Becker / *K. Curren*
1884	W. Renshaw / *H. F. Lawford*	★ 1907	N. E. Brookes / *A. W. Gore*	1934	F. J. Perry / *J. H. Crawford*	★ 1963	C. R. McKinley / *F. S. Stolle*	1986	B. Becker / *I. Lendl*
1885	W. Renshaw / *H. F. Lawford*	★ 1908	A. W. Gore / *H. Roper Barrett*	1935	F. J. Perry / *G. von Cramm*	1964	R. Emerson / *F. S. Stolle*	1987	P. Cash / *I. Lendl*
1886	W. Renshaw / *H. F. Lawford*	1909	A. W. Gore / *M. J. G. Ritchie*	1936	F. J. Perry / *G. von Cramm*	1965	R. Emerson / *F. S. Stolle*	1988	S. Edberg / *B. Becker*
★ 1887	H. F. Lawford / *E. Renshaw*	1910	A. F. Wilding / *A. W. Gore*	★ 1937	J. D. Budge / *G. von Cramm*	1966	M. Santana / *R. D. Ralston*	1989	B. Becker / *S. Edberg*
1888	E. Renshaw / *H. F. Lawford*	1911	A. F. Wilding / *H. Roper Barrett*	1938	J. D. Budge / *H. W. Austin*	1967	J. D. Newcombe / *W. P. Bungert*	1990	S. Edberg / *B. Becker*
1889	W. Renshaw / *E. Renshaw*	1912	A. F. Wilding / *A. W. Gore*	★ 1939	R. L. Riggs / *E. T. Cooke*	1968	R. Laver / *A. D. Roche*	1991	M. Stich / *B. Becker*
1890	W. J. Hamilton / *W. Renshaw*	1913	A. F. Wilding / *M. E. McLoughlin*	★ 1946	Y. Petra / *G. E. Brown*	1969	R. Laver / *J. D. Newcombe*	1992	A. Agassi / *G. Ivanisevic*
★ 1891	W. Baddeley / *J. Pim*	1914	N. E. Brookes / *A. F. Wilding*	1947	J. Kramer / *T. Brown*	1970	J. D. Newcombe / *K. R. Rosewall*	1993	P. Sampras / *J. Courier*
1892	W. Baddeley / *J. Pim*	1919	G. L. Patterson / *N. E. Brookes*	★ 1948	R. Falkenburg / *J. E. Bromwich*	1971	J. D. Newcombe / *S. R. Smith*	1994	P. Sampras / *G. Ivanisevic*
1893	J. Pim / *W. Baddeley*	1920	W. T. Tilden / *G. L. Patterson*	1949	F. R. Schroeder / *J. Drobny*	★ 1972	S. R. Smith / *I. Nastase*	1995	P. Sampras / *B. Becker*
1894	J. Pim / *W. Baddeley*	1921	W. T. Tilden / *B. I. C. Norton*	★ 1950	B. Patty / *F. A. Sedgman*	★ 1973	J. Kodes / *A. Metreveli*	1996	R. Krajicek / *M. Washington*
★ 1895	W. Baddeley / *W. V. Eaves*	★† 1922	G. L. Patterson / *R. Lycett*	1951	R. Savitt / *K. McGregor*	1974	J. S. Connors / *K. R. Rosewall*	1997	P. Sampras / *C. Pioline*
1896	H. S. Mahony / *W. Baddeley*	★ 1923	W. M. Johnston / *F. T. Hunter*	1952	F. A. Sedgman / *J. Drobny*	1975	A. R. Ashe / *J. S. Connors*	1998	P. Sampras / *G. Ivanisevic*
1897	R. F. Doherty / *H. S. Mahony*	★ 1924	J. Borotra / *R. Lacoste*	★ 1953	V. Seixas / *K. Nielsen*	1976	B. Borg / *I. Nastase*	1999	P. Sampras / *A. Agassi*
1898	R. F. Doherty / *H. L. Doherty*	1925	R. Lacoste / *J. Borotra*	1954	J. Drobny / *K. R. Rosewall*	1977	B. Borg / *J. S. Connors*	2000	P. Sampras / *P. Rafter*
1899	R. F. Doherty / *A. W. Gore*	1926	J. Borotra / *H. Kinsey*	1955	T. Trabert / *K. Nielsen*	1978	B. Borg / *J. S. Connors*		

NOTE: For the years 1913, 1914 and 1919–23 inclusive the Championship Roll includes the 'World's Championship on Grass' granted to The Lawn Tennis Association by The International Lawn Tennis Federation. This title was then abolished and commencing in 1924 they became The Official Lawn Tennis Championships recognised by The International Lawn Tennis Federation. Prior to 1922 the holders in the singles events and the gentlemen's doubles did not compete in The Championships but met the winners of these events in the Challenge Rounds.

† Challenge Round abolished; holders subsequently played through.   *The holder did not defend the title.

157

THE CHAMPIONSHIP ROLL – LADIES' SINGLES

Champions and Runners-up

Year	Champion / Runner-up	Year	Champion / Runner-up	Year	Champion / Runner-up	Year	Champion / Runner-up	Year	Champion / Runner-up
1884	Miss M. Watson / Miss L. Watson	1906	Miss D. K. Douglass / Miss M. Sutton	*1932	Mrs. F. S. Moody / Miss H. H. Jacobs	*1959	Miss M. E. Bueno / Miss D. R. Hard	1980	Mrs. R. Cawley / Mrs. J. M. Lloyd
1885	Miss M. Watson / Miss B. Bingley	1907	Miss M. Sutton / Mrs. Lambert Chambers	1933	Mrs. F. S. Moody / Miss D. E. Round	1960	Miss M. E. Bueno / Miss S. Reynolds	*1981	Mrs. J. M. Lloyd / Miss H. Mandlikova
1886	Miss B. Bingley / Miss M. Watson	*1908	Mrs. A. Sterry / Miss A. M. Morton	*1934	Miss D. E. Round / Miss H. H. Jacobs	*1961	Miss A. Mortimer / Miss C. C. Truman	1982	Miss M. Navratilova / Mrs. J. M. Lloyd
1887	Miss L. Dod / Miss B. Bingley	*1909	Miss D. P. Boothby / Miss A. M. Morton	1935	Mrs. F. S. Moody / Miss H. H. Jacobs	1962	Mrs. J. R. Susman / Mrs. V. Sukova	1983	Miss M. Navratilova / Miss A. Jaeger
1888	Miss L. Dod / Mrs. G. W. Hillyard	1910	Mrs. Lambert Chambers / Miss D. P. Boothby	*1936	Miss H. H. Jacobs / Frau. S. Sperling	*1963	Miss M. Smith / Miss B. J. Moffitt	1984	Miss M. Navratilova / Mrs. J. M. Lloyd
*1889	Mrs. G. W. Hillyard / Miss L. Rice	1911	Mrs. Lambert Chambers / Miss D. P. Boothby	1937	Miss D. E. Round / Miss J. Jedrzejowska	1964	Miss M. E. Bueno / Miss M. Smith	1985	Miss M. Navratilova / Mrs. J. M. Lloyd
*1890	Miss L. Rice / Miss M. Jacks	*1912	Mrs. D. R. Larcombe / Mrs. A. Sterry	*1938	Mrs. F. S. Moody / Miss H. H. Jacobs	1965	Miss M. Smith / Miss M. E. Bueno	1986	Miss M. Navratilova / Miss H. Mandlikova
*1891	Miss L. Dod / Mrs. G. W. Hillyard	*1913	Mrs. Lambert Chambers / Mrs. R. J. McNair	*1939	Miss A. Marble / Miss K. E. Stammers	1966	Mrs. L. W. King / Miss M. E. Bueno	1987	Miss M. Navratilova / Miss S. Graf
1892	Miss L. Dod / Mrs. G. W. Hillyard	1914	Mrs. Lambert Chambers / Mrs. D. R. Larcombe	*1946	Miss P. Betz / Miss L. Brough	1967	Mrs. L. W. King / Mrs. P. F. Jones	1988	Miss S. Graf / Miss M. Navratilova
1893	Miss L. Dod / Mrs. G. W. Hillyard	1919	Mlle. S. Lenglen / Mrs. Lambert Chambers	*1947	Miss M. Osborne / Miss D. Hart	1968	Mrs. L. W. King / Miss J. A. M. Tegart	1989	Miss S. Graf / Miss M. Navratilova
*1894	Mrs. G. W. Hillyard / Miss E. L. Austin	1920	Mlle. S. Lenglen / Mrs. Lambert Chambers	1948	Miss L. Brough / Miss D. Hart	1969	Mrs. P. F. Jones / Mrs. L. W. King	1990	Miss M. Navratilova / Miss Z. Garrison
*1895	Miss C. Cooper / Miss H. Jackson	1921	Mlle. S. Lenglen / Miss E. Ryan	1949	Miss L. Brough / Mrs. W. du Pont	*1970	Mrs. B. M. Court / Mrs. L. W. King	1991	Miss S. Graf / Miss G. Sabatini
1896	Miss C. Cooper / Mrs. W. H. Pickering	†1922	Mlle. S. Lenglen / Mrs. F. Mallory	1950	Miss L. Brough / Mrs. W. du Pont	1971	Miss E. F. Goolagong / Mrs. B. M. Court	1992	Miss S. Graf / Miss M. Seles
1897	Mrs. G. W. Hillyard / Miss C. Cooper	1923	Mlle. S. Lenglen / Miss K. McKane	1951	Miss D. Hart / Miss S. Fry	1972	Mrs. L. W. King / Miss E. F. Goolagong	1993	Miss S. Graf / Miss J. Novotna
*1898	Miss C. Cooper / Miss L Martin	1924	Miss K. McKane / Miss H. Wills	1952	Miss M. Connolly / Miss L. Brough	1973	Mrs. L. W. King / Miss C. M. Evert	1994	Miss C. Martinez / Miss M. Navratilova
1899	Mrs. G. W. Hillyard / Miss C. Cooper	1925	Mlle. S. Lenglen / Miss J. Fry	1953	Miss M. Connolly / Miss D. Hart	1974	Miss C. M. Evert / Mrs. O. Morozova	1995	Miss S. Graf / Miss A. Sanchez Vicario
1900	Mrs. G. W. Hillyard / Miss C. Cooper	1926	Mrs. L. A. Godfree / Sta. L. de Alvarez	1954	Miss M. Connolly / Miss L. Brough	1975	Mrs. L. W. King / Mrs. R. Cawley	1996	Miss S. Graf / Miss A. Sanchez Vicario
1901	Mrs. A. Sterry / Mrs. G. W. Hillyard	1927	Miss H. Wills / Sta. L. de Alvarez	*1955	Miss L. Brough / Mrs. J. G. Fleitz	*1976	Miss C. M. Evert / Mrs. R. Cawley	*1997	Miss M. Hingis / Miss J. Novotna
1902	Miss M. E. Robb / Mrs. A. Sterry	1928	Miss H. Wills / Sta. L. de Alvarez	1956	Miss S. Fry / Miss A. Buxton	1977	Miss S. V. Wade / Miss B. F. Stove	1998	Miss J. Novotna / Miss N. Tauziat
*1903	Miss D. K. Douglass / Miss E. W. Thomson	1929	Miss H. Wills / Miss H. H. Jacobs	*1957	Miss A. Gibson / Miss D. R. Hard	1978	Miss M. Navratilova / Miss C. M. Evert	1999	Miss L. A. Davenport / Miss S. Graf
1904	Miss D. K. Douglass / Mrs. A. Sterry	1930	Mrs. F. S. Moody / Miss E. Ryan	1958	Miss A. Gibson / Miss A. Mortimer	1979	Miss M. Navratilova / Mrs. J. M. Lloyd	2000	Miss V. Williams / Miss L. A. Davenport
1905	Miss M. Sutton / Miss D. K. Douglass	*1931	Fraulein C. Aussem / Fraulein H. Krahwinkel						

MAIDEN NAMES OF LADY CHAMPIONS

In the tables the following have been recorded in both married and single identities.

Mrs. R. Cawley .... Miss E. F. Goolagong
Mrs. Lambert Chambers .... Miss D. K. Douglass
Mrs. B. M. Court .... Miss M. Smith
Mrs. B. C. Covell .... Miss P. L. Howkins
Mrs. D. E. Dalton .... Miss J. A. M. Tegart
Mrs. W. du Pont .... Miss M. Osborne
Mrs. L. A. Godfree .... Miss K. McKane
Mrs. H. F. Gourlay Cawley .... Miss H. F. Gourlay

Mrs. G. W. Hillyard .... Miss B. Bingley
Mrs. P. F. Jones .... Miss A. S. Haydon
Mrs. L. W. King .... Miss B. J. Moffitt
Mrs. M. R. King .... Miss P. E. Mudford
Mrs. D. R. Larcombe .... Miss E. W. Thomson
Mrs. J. M. Lloyd .... Miss C. M. Evert

Mrs. F. S. Moody .... Miss H. Wills
Mrs. O. Morozova .... Miss O. Morozova
Mrs. L. E. G. Price .... Miss S. Reynolds
Mrs. G. E. Reid .... Miss K. Melville
Mrs. P. D. Smylie .... Miss E. M. Sayers
Frau. S. Sperling .... Fraulein H. Krahwinkel
Mrs. A. Sterry .... Miss C. Cooper
Mrs. J. R. Susman .... Miss K. Hantze

GENTLEMEN'S DOUBLES

1879 L. R. Erskine and H. F. Lawford
F. Durant and G. E. Tabor
1880 W. Renshaw and E. Renshaw
O. E. Woodhouse and C. J. Cole
1881 W. Renshaw and E. Renshaw
W. J. Down and H. Vaughan
1882 J. T. Hartley and R. T. Richardson
J. G. Horn and C. B. Russell
1883 C. W. Grinstead and C. E. Welldon
C. B. Russell and R. T. Milford
1884 W. Renshaw and E. Renshaw
E. W. Lewis and E. L. Williams
1885 W. Renshaw and E. Renshaw
C. E. Farrer and A. J. Stanley
1886 W. Renshaw and E. Renshaw
C. E. Farrer and A. J. Stanley
1887 P. Bowes-Lyon and H. W. W. Wilberforce
J. H. Crispe and E. Barratt Smith
1888 W. Renshaw and E. Renshaw
P. Bowes-Lyon and H. W. W. Wilberforce
1889 W. Renshaw and E. Renshaw
E. W. Lewis and G. W. Hillyard
1890 J. Pim and F. O. Stoker
E. W. Lewis and G. W. Hillyard
1891 W. Baddeley and H. Baddeley
J. Pim and F. O. Stoker
1892 H. S. Barlow and E. W. Lewis
W. Baddeley and H. Baddeley
1893 J. Pim and F. O. Stoker
E. W. Lewis and H. S. Barlow
1894 W. Baddeley and H. Baddeley
H. S. Barlow and C. H. Martin
1895 W. Baddeley and H. Baddeley
E. W. Lewis and W. V. Eaves
1896 W. Baddeley and H. Baddeley
R. F. Doherty and H. A. Nisbet
1897 R. F. Doherty and H. L. Doherty
W. Baddeley and H. Baddeley
1898 R. F. Doherty and H. L. Doherty
H. A. Nisbet and C. Hobart
1899 R. F. Doherty and H. L. Doherty
H. A. Nisbet and C. Hobart
1900 R. F. Doherty and H. L. Doherty
H. Roper Barrett and H. A. Nisbet
1901 R. F. Doherty and H. L. Doherty
Dwight Davis and Holcombe Ward
1902 S. H. Smith and F. L. Riseley
R. F. Doherty and H. L. Doherty
1903 R. F. Doherty and H. L. Doherty
S. H. Smith and F. L. Riseley
1904 R. F. Doherty and H. L. Doherty
S. H. Smith and F. L. Riseley
1905 R. F. Doherty and H. L. Doherty
S. H. Smith and F. L. Riseley
1906 S. H. Smith and F. L. Riseley
R. F. Doherty and H. L. Doherty
1907 N. E. Brooks and A. F. Wilding
B. C. Wright and K. H. Behr
1908 A. F. Wilding and M. J. G. Ritchie
A. W. Gore and H. Roper Barrett
1909 A. W. Gore and H. Roper Barrett
S. N. Doust and H. A. Parker
1910 A. F. Wilding and M. J. G. Ritchie
A. W. Gore and H. Roper Barrett
1911 M. Decugis and A. H. Gobert
M. J. G. Ritchie and A. F. Wilding
1912 H. Roper Barrett and C. P. Dixon
M. Decugis and A. H. Gobert
1913 H. Roper Barrett and C. P. Dixon
F. W. Rahe and H. Kleinschroth
1914 N. E. Brookes and A. F. Wilding
H. Roper Barrett and C. P. Dixon
1919 R. V. Thomas and P. O'Hara-Wood
R. Lycett and R. W. Heath
1920 R. N. Williams and C. S. Garland
A. R. F. Kingscote and J. C. Parke
1921 R. Lycett and M. Woosnam
F. G. Lowe and A. H. Lowe
1922 R. Lycett and J. O. Anderson
G. L. Patterson and P. O'Hara-Wood
1923 R. Lycett and L. A. Godfree
Count de Gomar and E. Flaquer
1924 F. T. Hunter and V. Richards
R. N. Williams and W. M. Washburn
1925 J. Borotra and R. Lacoste
J. Hennessey and R. Casey
1926 H. Cochet and J. Brugnon
V. Richards and H. Kinsey
1927 F. T. Hunter and W. T. Tilden
J. Brugnon and H. Cochet
1928 H. Cochet and J. Brugnon
G. L. Patterson and J. B. Hawkes
1929 W. Allison and J. Van Ryn
J. C. Gregory and I. G. Collins
1930 W. Allison and J. Van Ryn
J. H. Doeg and G. M. Lott
1931 G. M Lott and J. Van Ryn
H. Cochet and J. Brugnon
1932 J. Borotra and J. Brugnon
G. P. Hughes and F. J. Perry
1933 J. Borotra and J. Brugnon
R. Nunoi and J. Satoh
1934 G. M. Lott and L. R. Stoefen
J. Borotra and J. Brugnon
1935 J. H. Crawford and A. K. Quist
W. Allison and J. Van Ryn
1936 G. P. Hughes and C. R. D. Tuckey
C. E. Hare and F. H. D. Wilde
1937 J. D. Budge and G. Mako
G. P. Hughes and C. R. D. Tuckey
1938 J. D. Budge and G. Mako
H. Henkel and G. von Metaxa
1939 R. L. Riggs and E. T. Cooke
C. E. Hare and F. H. D. Wilde
1946 T. Brown and J. Kramer
G. E. Brown and D. Pails
1947 R. Falkenburg and J. Kramer
A. J. Mottram and O. W. Sidwell
1948 J. E. Bromwich and F. A. Sedgman
T. Brown and G. Mulloy
1949 R. Gonzales and F. Parker
G. Mulloy and F. R. Schroeder
1950 J. E. Bromwich and A. K. Quist
G. E. Brown and O. W. Sidwell
1951 K. McGregor and F. A. Sedgman
J. Drobny and E. W. Sturgess
1952 K. McGregor and F. A. Sedgman
V. Seixas and E. W. Sturgess
1953 L. A. Hoad and K. R. Rosewall
R. N. Hartwig and M. G. Rose
1954 R. N. Hartwig and M. G. Rose
V. Seixas and T. Trabert
1955 R. N. Hartwig and L. A. Hoad
N. A. Fraser and K. R. Rosewall
1956 L. A. Hoad and K. R. Rosewall
N. Pietrangeli and O. Sirola
1957 G. Mulloy and B. Patty
N. A. Fraser and L. A. Hoad
1958 S. Davidson and U. Schmidt
A. J. Cooper and N. A. Fraser
1959 R. Emerson and N. A. Fraser
R. Laver and R. Mark
1960 R. H. Osuna and R. D. Ralston
M. G. Davies and R. K. Wilson
1961 R. Emerson and N. A. Fraser
R. A. J. Hewitt and F. S. Stolle
1962 R. A. J. Hewitt and F. S. Stolle
B. Jovanovic and N. Pilic
1963 R. H. Osuna and A. Palafox
J. C. Barclay and P. Darmon
1964 R. A. J. Hewitt and F. S. Stolle
R. Emerson and K. N. Fletcher
1965 J. D. Newcombe and A. D. Roche
K. N. Fletcher and R. A. J. Hewitt
1966 K. N. Fletcher and J. D. Newcombe
W. W. Bowrey and O. K. Davidson
1967 R. A. J. Hewitt and F. D. McMillan
R. Emerson and K. N. Fletcher
1968 J. D. Newcombe and A. D. Roche
K. R. Rosewall and F. S. Stolle
1969 J. D. Newcombe and A. D. Roche
T. S. Okker and M. C. Reissen
1970 J. D. Newcombe and A. D. Roche
K. R. Rosewall and F. S. Stolle
1971 R. S. Emerson and R. G. Laver
A. R. Ashe and R. D. Ralston
1972 R. A. J. Hewitt and F. D. McMillan
S. R. Smith and E. J. van Dillen
1973 J. S. Connors and I. Nastase
J. R. Cooper and N. A. Fraser
1974 J. D. Newcombe and A. D. Roche
R. C. Lutz and S. R. Smith
1975 V. Gerulaitis and A. Mayer
C. Dowdeswell and A. J. Stone
1976 B. E. Gottfried and R. Ramirez
R. L. Case and G. Masters
1977 R. L. Case and G. Masters
J. G. Alexander and P. C. Dent
1978 R. A. J. Hewitt and F. D. McMillan
P. Fleming and J. P. McEnroe
1979 P. Fleming and J. P. McEnroe
B. E. Gottfried and R. Ramirez
1980 P. McNamara and P. McNamee
R. C. Lutz and S. R. Smith
1981 P. Fleming and J. P. McEnroe
R. C. Lutz and S. R. Smith
1982 P. McNamara and P. McNamee
P. Fleming and J. P. McEnroe
1983 P. Fleming and J. P. McEnroe
T. E. Gullikson and T. R. Gullikson
1984 P. Fleming and J. P. McEnroe
P. Cash and P. McNamee
1985 H. P. Guenthardt and B. Taroczy
P. Cash and J. B. Fitzgerald
1986 J. Nystrom and M. Wilander
G. Donnelly and P. Fleming
1987 K. Flach and R. Seguso
S. Casal and E. Sanchez
1988 K. Flach and R. Seguso
J. B. Fitzgerald and A. Jarryd
1989 J. B. Fitzgerald and A. Jarryd
R. Leach and J. Pugh
1990 R. Leach and J. Pugh
P. Aldrich and D. T. Visser
1991 J. B. Fitzgerald and A. Jarryd
J. Frana and L. Lavalle
1992 J. P. McEnroe and M. Stich
J. Grabb and R. A. Reneberg
1993 T. A. Woodbridge and M. Woodforde
G. Connell and P. Galbraith
1994 T. A. Woodbridge and M. Woodforde
G. Connell and P. Galbraith
1995 T. A. Woodbridge and M. Woodforde
R. Leach and S. Melville
1996 T. A. Woodbridge and M. Woodforde
B. Black and G. Connell
1997 T. A. Woodbridge and M. Woodforde
J. Eltingh and P. Haarhuis
1998 J. Eltingh and P. Haarhuis
T. A. Woodbridge and M. Woodforde
1999 M. Bhupathi and L. Paes
P. Haarhuis and J. Palmer
2000 T. A. Woodbridge and M. Woodforde
P. Haarhuis and S. Stolle

LADIES' DOUBLES

1913 Mrs. R. J. McNair and Miss D. P. Boothby
Mrs. A. Sterry and Mrs. Lambert Chambers
1914 Miss E. Ryan and Miss A. M. Morton
Mrs. D. R. Larcombe and Mrs. F. J. Hannam
1919 Mlle. S. Lenglen and Miss E. Ryan
Mrs. Lambert Chambers and Mrs. D. R. Larcombe
1920 Mlle. S. Lenglen and Miss E. Ryan
Mrs. Lambert Chambers and Mrs. D. R. Larcombe
1921 Mlle. S. Lenglen and Miss E. Ryan
Mrs. A. E. Beamish and Mrs. G. E. Peacock
1922 Mlle. S. Lenglen and Miss E. Ryan
Mrs. A. D. Stocks and Miss K. McKane
1923 Mlle. S. Lenglen and Miss E. Ryan
Miss J. Austin and Miss E. L. Colyer
1924 Mrs. H. Wightman and Miss H. Wills
Mrs. B. C. Covell and Miss K. McKane
1925 Mlle. S. Lenglen and Miss E. Ryan
Mrs. A. V. Bridge and Mrs. C. G. McIlquham
1926 Miss E. Ryan and Miss M. K. Browne
Mrs. L. A. Godfree and Miss E. L. Colyer
1927 Miss H. Wills and Miss E. Ryan
Miss E. L. Heine and Mrs. G. E. Peacock
1928 Mrs. Holcroft-Watson and Miss P. Saunders
Miss E. H. Harvey and Miss E. Bennett
1929 Mrs. Holcroft-Watson and Mrs. L.R.C. Michell
Mrs. B. C. Covell and Mrs. D. C. Shepherd-Barron
1930 Mrs. F. S. Moody and Miss E. Ryan
Miss E. Cross and Miss S. Palfrey
1931 Mrs.D.C. Shepherd-Barron and Miss P.E. Mudford
Mlle. D. Metaxa and Mlle. J. Sigart
1932 Mlle. D. Metaxa and Mlle. J. Sigart
Miss E. Ryan and Miss H. H. Jacobs
1933 Mme. R. Mathieu and Miss E. Ryan
Miss F. James and Miss A. M. Yorke
1934 Mme. R. Mathieu and Miss E. Ryan
Mrs. D. Andrus and Mme. S. Henrotin
1935 Miss F. James and Miss K. E. Stammers
Mme. R. Mathieu and Frau. S. Sperling
1936 Miss F. James and Miss K. E. Stammers
Mrs. S. P. Fabyan and Miss H. H. Jacobs
1937 Mme. R. Mathieu and Miss A. M. Yorke
Mrs. M. R. King and Mrs. J. B. Pittman
1938 Mrs. S. P. Fabyan and Miss A. Marble
Mme. R. Mathieu and Miss A. M. Yorke
1939 Mrs S. P. Fabyan and Miss A. Marble
Miss H. H. Jacobs and Miss A. M. Yorke
1946 Miss L. Brough and Miss M. Osborne
Miss P. Betz and Miss D. Hart
1947 Miss D. Hart and Mrs. P. C. Todd
Miss L. Brough and Miss M. Osborne
1948 Miss L. Brough and Mrs. W. du Pont
Miss D. Hart and Mrs. P. C. Todd
1949 Miss L. Brough and Mrs. W. du Pont
Miss G. Moran and Mrs. P. C. Todd
1950 Miss L. Brough and Mrs. W. du Pont
Miss S. Fry and Miss D. Hart
1951 Miss S. Fry and Miss D. Hart
Miss L. Brough and Mrs. W. du Pont
1952 Miss S. Fry and Miss D. Hart
Miss L. Brough and Miss M. Connolly
1953 Miss S. Fry and Miss D. Hart
Miss M. Connolly and Miss J. Sampson
1954 Miss L. Brough and Mrs. W. du Pont
Miss S. Fry and Miss D. Hart
1955 Miss A. Mortimer and Miss J. A. Shilcock
Miss S. J. Bloomer and Miss P. E. Ward
1956 Miss A. Buxton and Miss A. Gibson
Miss F. Muller and Miss D. G. Seeney
1957 Miss A. Gibson and Miss D. R. Hard
Mrs. K. Hawton and Mrs. T. D. Long
1958 Miss M. E. Bueno and Miss A. Gibson
Mrs. W. du Pont and Miss M. Varner
1959 Miss J. Arth and Miss D. R. Hard
Mrs. J. G. Fleitz and Miss C. C. Truman
1960 Miss M. E. Bueno and Miss D. R. Hard
Miss S. Reynolds and Miss R. Schuurman
1961 Miss K. Hantze and Miss B. J. Moffitt
Miss J. Lehane and Miss M. Smith
1962 Miss B. J. Moffitt and Mrs. J. R. Susman
Mrs. L. E. G. Price and Miss R. Schuurman
1963 Miss M. E. Bueno and Miss D. R. Hard
Miss R. A. Ebbern and Miss M. Smith
1964 Miss M. Smith and Miss L. R. Turner
Miss B. J. Moffitt and Mrs. J. R. Susman
1965 Miss M. E. Bueno and Miss B. J. Moffitt
Miss F. Durr and Miss J. Lieffrig
1966 Miss M. E. Bueno and Miss N. Richey
Miss M. Smith and Miss J. A. M. Tegart
1967 Miss R. Casals and Mrs. L. W. King
Miss M. E. Bueno and Miss N. Richey
1968 Miss R. Casals and Mrs. L. W. King
Miss F. Durr and Mrs. P. F. Jones
1969 Mrs. B. M. Court and Miss J. A. M. Tegart
Miss P. S. A. Hogan and Miss M. Michel
1970 Miss R. Casals and Mrs. L. W. King
Miss F. Durr and Miss S. V. Wade
1971 Miss R. Casals and Mrs. L. W. King
Mrs. B. M. Court and Miss E. F. Goolagong
1972 Mrs. L. W. King and Miss B. F. Stove
Mrs. D. E. Dalton and Miss F. Durr
1973 Miss R. Casals and Mrs. L. W. King
Miss F. Durr and Miss B. F. Stove
1974 Miss E. F. Goolagong and Miss M. Michel
Miss H. F. Gourlay and Miss K. M. Krantzcke
1975 Miss A. Kiyomura and Miss K. Sawamatsu
Miss F. Durr and Miss B. F. Stove
1976 Miss C. M. Evert and Miss M. Navratilova
Mrs. L. W. King and Miss B. F. Stove
1977 Mrs. H. F. Gourlay Cawley and Miss J. C. Russell
Miss M. Navratilova and Miss B. F. Stove
1978 Mrs. G. E. Reid and Miss. W. M. Turnbull
Miss M. Jausovec and Miss V. Ruzici
1979 Mrs. L. W. King and Miss M. Navratilova
Miss B. F. Stove and Miss W. M. Turnbull
1980 Miss K. Jordan and Miss A. E. Smith
Miss R. Casals and Miss W. M. Turnbull
1981 Miss M. Navratilova and Miss P. H. Shriver
Miss K. Jordan and Miss A. E. Smith
1982 Miss M. Navratilova and Miss P. H. Shriver
Miss K. Jordan and Miss A. E. Smith
1983 Miss M. Navratilova and Miss P. H. Shriver
Miss R. Casals and Miss W. M. Turnbull
1984 Miss M. Navratilova and Miss P. H. Shriver
Miss K. Jordan and Miss A. E. Smith
1985 Miss K. Jordan and Mrs. P. D. Smylie
Miss M. Navratilova and Miss P. H. Shriver
1986 Miss M. Navratilova and Miss P. H. Shriver
Miss H. Mandlikova and Miss W. M. Turnbull
1987 Miss C. Kohde-Kilsch and Miss H. Sukova
Miss B. Nagelsen and Mrs. P. D. Smylie
1988 Miss S. Graf and Miss G. Sabatini
Miss L. Savchenko and Miss N. Zvereva
1989 Miss J. Novotna and Miss H. Sukova
Miss L. Savchenko and Miss N. Zvereva
1990 Miss J. Novotna and Miss H. Sukova
Miss K. Jordan and Mrs. P. D. Smylie
1991 Miss L. Savchenko and Miss N. Zvereva
Miss G. Fernandez and Miss J. Novotna
1992 Miss G. Fernandez and Miss N. Zvereva
Miss J. Novotna and Mrs. L. Savchenko-Neiland
1993 Miss G. Fernandez and Miss N. Zvereva
Mrs. L. Neiland and Miss J. Novotna
1994 Miss G. Fernandez and Miss N. Zvereva
Miss J. Novotna and Miss A. Sanchez Vicario
1995 Miss J. Novotna and Miss A. Sanchez Vicario
Miss G. Fernandez and Miss N. Zvereva
1996 Miss M. Hingis and Miss H. Sukova
Miss M.J. McGrath and Mrs. L. Neiland
1997 Miss G. Fernandez and Miss N. Zvereva
Miss N.J. Arendt and Miss M.M. Bollegraf
1998 Miss M. Hingis and Miss J. Novotna
Miss L.A. Davenport and Miss N. Zvereva
1999 Miss L.A. Davenport and Miss C. Morariu
Miss M. de Swardt and Miss E. Tatarkova
2000 Miss S. Williams and Miss V. Williams
Mrs J. Halard–Decugis and Miss A. Sugiyama

MIXED DOUBLES

1913 Hope Crisp and Mrs. C. O. Tuckey *J. C. Parke and Mrs. D. R. Larcombe*	1937 J. D. Budge and Miss A. Marble *Y. Petra and Mme. R. Mathieu*	1963 K. N. Fletcher and Miss M. Smith *R. A. J. Hewitt and Miss D. R. Hard*	1983 J. M. Lloyd and Miss W. M. Turnbull *S. Denton and Mrs. L. W. King*
1914 J. C. Parke and Mrs. D.R. Larcombe *A. F. Wilding and Mlle. M. Broquedis*	1938 J. D. Budge and Miss A. Marble *H. Henkel and Mrs. S. P. Fabyan*	1964 F. S. Stolle and Miss L. R. Turner *K. N. Fletcher and Miss M. Smith*	1984 J. M. Lloyd and Miss W. M. Turnbull *S. Denton and Miss K. Jordan*
1919 R. Lycett and Miss E. Ryan *A. D. Prebble and Mrs. Lambert Chambers*	1939 R. L. Riggs and Miss A. Marble *F. H. D. Wilde and Miss N. B. Brown*	1965 K. N. Fletcher and Miss M. Smith *A. D. Roche and Miss J. A. M. Tegart*	1985 P. McNamee and Miss M. Navratilova *J. B. Fitzgerald and Mrs. P. D. Smylie*
1920 G. L. Patterson and Mlle. S. Lenglen *R. Lycett and Miss E. Ryan*	1946 T. Brown and Miss L. Brough *G. E. Brown and Mrs. D. Bundy*	1966 K. N. Fletcher and Miss M. Smith *R. D. Ralston and Miss L. W. King*	1986 K. Flach and Miss K. Jordan *H. P. Guenthardt and Miss M. Navratilova*
1921 R. Lycett and Miss E. Ryan *M. Woosnam and Miss P. L. Howkins*	1947 J. E. Bromwich and Miss L. Brough *C. F. Long and Mrs. N. M. Bolton*	1967 O. K. Davidson and Mrs. L. W. King *K. N. Fletcher and Miss M. E. Bueno*	1987 M. J. Bates and Miss J. M. Durie *D. Cahill and Miss N. Provis*
1922 P. O'Hara-Wood and Mlle. S. Lenglen *R. Lycett and Miss E. Ryan*	1948 J. E. Bromwich and Miss L. Brough *F. A. Sedgman and Miss D. Hart*	1968 K. N. Fletcher and Mrs. B. M. Court *A. Metreveli and Miss O. Morozova*	1988 S. E. Stewart and Miss Z. L. Garrison *K. Jones and Mrs. S. W. Magers*
1923 R. Lycett and Miss E. Ryan *L. S. Deane and Mrs. D. C. Shepherd-Barron*	1949 E. W. Sturgess and Mrs. S. P. Summers *J. E. Bromwich and Miss L. Brough*	1969 F. S. Stolle and Mrs. P. F. Jones *A. D. Roche and Miss J. A. M. Tegart*	1989 J. Pugh and Miss J. Novotna *M. Kratzmann and Miss J. M. Byrne*
1924 J. B. Gilbert and Miss K. McKane *L. A. Godfree and Mrs. D. C. Shepherd-Barron*	1950 E. W. Sturgess and Miss L. Brough *G. E. Brown and Mrs. P. C. Todd*	1970 I. Nastase and Miss R. Casals *A. Metreveli and Miss O. Morozova*	1990 R. Leach and Miss Z. L. Garrison *J. B. Fitzgerald and Mrs P. D. Smylie*
1925 J. Borotra and Mlle. S. Lenglen *H. L. de Morpurgo and Miss E. Ryan*	1951 F. A. Sedgman and Miss D. Hart *M. G. Rose and Mrs. N. M. Bolton*	1971 O. K. Davidson and Mrs. L. W. King *M. C. Riessen and Mrs. B. M. Court*	1991 J. B. Fitzgerald and Mrs. P. D. Smylie *J. Pugh and Miss N. Zvereva*
1926 L. A. Godfree and Mrs. L. A. Godfree *H. Kinsey and Miss M. K. Browne*	1952 F. A. Sedgman and Miss D. Hart *E. Morea and Mrs. T. D. Long*	1972 I. Nastase and Miss R. Casals *K. G. Warwick and Miss E. F. Goolagong*	1992 C. Suk and Mrs L. Savchenko-Neiland *J. Eltingh and Miss M. Oremans*
1927 F. T. Hunter and Miss E. Ryan *L. A. Godfree and Mrs. L. A. Godfree*	1953 V. Seixas and Miss D. Hart *E. Morea and Miss S. Fry*	1973 O. K. Davidson and Mrs. L. W. King *R. Ramirez and Miss J. S. Newberry*	1993 M. Woodforde and Miss M. Navratilova *T. Nijssen and Miss M. M. Bollegraf*
1928 P. D. B. Spence and Miss E. Ryan *J. Crawford and Miss D. Akhurst*	1954 V. Seixas and Miss D. Hart *K. R. Rosewall and Mrs. W. du Pont*	1974 O. K. Davidson and Mrs. L. W. King *M. J. Farrell and Miss L. J. Charles*	1994 T. A. Woodbridge and Miss H. Sukova *T. J. Middleton and Miss L. M. McNeil*
1929 F. T. Hunter and Miss H. Wills *I. G. Collins and Miss J. Fry*	1955 V. Seixas and Miss D. Hart *E. Morea and Miss L. Brough*	1975 M. C. Riessen and Mrs. B. M. Court *A. J. Stone and Miss B. F. Stove*	1995 J. Stark and Miss M. Navratilova *C. Suk and Miss G. Fernandez*
1930 J. H. Crawford and Miss E. Ryan *D. Prenn and Fraulein H. Krahwinkel*	1956 V. Seixas and Miss S. Fry *G. Mulloy and Miss A. Gibson*	1976 A. D. Roche and Miss F. Durr *R. L. Stockton and Miss R. Casals*	1996 C. Suk and Miss H. Sukova *M. Woodforde and Mrs. L. Neiland*
1931 G. M. Lott and Mrs L. A. Harper *I. G. Collins and Miss J. C. Ridley*	1957 M. G. Rose and Miss D. R. Hard *N. A. Fraser and Miss A. Gibson*	1977 R. A. J. Hewitt and Miss G. R. Stevens *F. D. McMillan and Miss B. F. Stove*	1997 C. Suk and Miss H. Sukova *A. Olhovskiy and Mrs L. Neiland*
1932 E. Maier and Miss E. Ryan *H. C. Hopman and Mlle. J. Sigart*	1958 R. N. Howe and Miss L. Coghlan *K. Nielsen and Miss A. Gibson*	1978 F. D. McMillan and Miss B. F. Stove *R. O. Ruffels and Mrs. L. W. King*	1998 M. Mirnyi and Miss S. Williams *M. Bhupathi and Miss M. Lucic*
1933 G. von Cramm and Fraulein H. Krahwinkel *N. G. Farquharson and Miss M. Heeley*	1959 R. Laver and Miss D. R. Hard *N. A. Fraser and Miss M. E. Bueno*	1979 R. A. J. Hewitt and Miss G. R. Stevens *F. D. McMillan and Miss B. F. Stove*	1999 L. Paes and Miss L.M. Raymond *J. Bjorkman and Miss A. Kournikova*
1934 R. Miki and Miss D. E. Round *H. W. Austin and Mrs D. C. Shepherd-Barron*	1960 R. Laver and Miss D. R. Hard *R. N. Howe and Miss M. E. Bueno*	1980 J. R. Austin and Miss T. Austin *M. R. Edmondson and Miss D. L. Fromholtz*	2000 D. Johnson and Miss K. Po *L. Hewitt and Miss K. Clijsters*
1935 F. J. Perry and Miss D. E. Round *H. C. Hopman and Mrs. H. C. Hopman*	1961 F. S. Stolle and Miss L. R. Turner *R. N. Howe and Miss E. Buding*	1981 F. D. McMillan and Miss B. F. Stove *J. R. Austin and Miss T. Austin*	
1936 F. J. Perry and Miss D. E. Round *J. D. Budge and Mrs. S. P. Fabyan*	1962 N. A. Fraser and Mrs. W. du Pont *R. D. Ralston and Miss A. S. Haydon*	1982 K. Curren and Miss A. E. Smith *J. M. Lloyd and Miss W. M. Turnbull*	

THE JUNIOR CHAMPIONSHIP ROLL

BOYS' SINGLES

1947 K. Nielsen (Denmark)	1961 C. E. Graebner (U.S.A.)	1975 C. J. Lewis (N.Z.)	1989 N. Kulti (Sweden)
1948 S. Stockenberg (Sweden)	1962 S. Matthews (G.B.)	1976 H. Guenthardt (Switzerland)	1990 L. Paes (India)
1949 S. Stockenberg (Sweden)	1963 N. Kalogeropoulos (Greece)	1977 V. A. Winitsky (U.S.A.)	1991 T. Enquist (Sweden)
1950 J. A. T. Horn (G.B.)	1964 I. El Shafei (U.A.R.)	1978 I. Lendl (Czechoslovakia)	1992 D. Skoch (Czechoslovakia)
1951 J. Kupferburger (S.A.)	1965 V. Korotkov (U.S.S.R.)	1979 R. Krishnan (India)	1993 R. Sabau (Romania)
1952 R. K. Wilson (G.B.)	1966 V. Korotkov (U.S.S.R.)	1980 T. Tulasne (France)	1994 S. Humphries (U.S.A.)
1953 W. A. Knight (G.B.)	1967 M. Orantes (Spain)	1981 M. W. Anger (U.S.A.)	1995 O. Mutis (France)
1954 R. Krishnan (India)	1968 J. G. Alexander (Australia)	1982 P. Cash (Australia)	1996 V. Voltchkov (Belarus)
1955 M. P. Hann (G.B.)	1969 B. Bertram (S.A.)	1983 S. Edberg (Sweden)	1997 W. Whitehouse (South Africa)
1956 R. Holmberg (U.S.A.)	1970 B. Bertram (S.A.)	1984 M. Kratzmann (Australia)	1998 R. Federer (Switzerland)
1957 J. I. Tattersall (G.B.)	1971 R. Kreiss (U.S.A.)	1985 L. Lavalle (Mexico)	1999 J. Melzer (Austria)
1958 E. Buchholz (U.S.A.)	1972 B. Borg (Sweden)	1986 E. Velez (Mexico)	2000 N. Mahut (France)
1959 T. Lejus (U.S.S.R.)	1973 W. Martin (U.S.A.)	1987 D. Nargiso (Italy)	
1960 A. R. Mandelstam (S.A.)	1974 W. Martin (U.S.A.)	1988 N. Pereira (Venezuela)	

BOYS' DOUBLES

1982 P. Cash and J. Frawley	1987 J. Stoltenberg and T. Woodbridge	1992 S. Baldas and S. Draper	1997 L. Horna and N. Massu
1983 M. Kratzmann and S. Youl	1988 J. Stoltenberg and T. Woodbridge	1993 S. Downs and J. Greenhalgh	1998 R. Federer and O. Rochus
1984 R. Brown and R. Weiss	1989 J. Palmer and J. Stark	1994 B. Ellwood and M. Philippoussis	1999 G. Coria and D. Nalbandian
1985 A. Moreno and J. Yzaga	1990 S. Lareau and S. Leblanc	1995 M. Lee and J.M. Trotman	2000 D. Coene and K. Vliegen
1986 T. Carbonell and P. Korda	1991 K. Alami and G. Rusedski	1996 D. Bracciali and J. Robichaud	

GIRLS' SINGLES

1947 Miss B. Domken (Belgium)	1961 Miss G. Baksheeva (U.S.S.R.)	1975 Miss N.Y. Chmyreva (U.S.S.R.)	1989 Miss A. Strnadova (Czechoslavakia)
1948 Miss O. Miskova (Czechoslovakia)	1962 Miss G. Baksheeva (U.S.S.R.)	1976 Miss N.Y. Chmyreva (U.S.S.R.)	1990 Miss A. Strnadova (Czechoslavakia)
1949 Miss S. Mercelis (Belgium)	1963 Miss D. M. Salfati (France)	1977 Miss L. Antonoplis (U.S.A.)	1991 Miss B. Rittner (Germany)
1950 Miss L. Cornell (G.B.)	1964 Miss P. Bartkowicz (U.S.A.)	1978 Miss T. Austin (U.S.A.)	1992 Miss C. Rubin (U.S.A.)
1951 Miss L. Cornell (G.B.)	1965 Miss O. Morozova (U.S.S.R.)	1979 Miss M. L. Piatek (U.S.A.)	1993 Miss N. Feber (Belgium)
1952 Miss ten Bosch (Netherlands)	1966 Miss B. Lindstrom (Finland)	1980 Miss D. Freeman (Australia)	1994 Miss M. Hingis (Switzerland)
1953 Miss D. Kilian (S.A.)	1967 Miss J. Salome (Netherlands)	1981 Miss Z. Garrison (U.S.A.)	1995 Miss A. Olsza (Poland)
1954 Miss V. A. Pitt (G.B.)	1968 Miss K. Pigeon (U.S.A.)	1982 Miss C. Tanvier (France)	1996 Miss A. Mauresmo (France)
1955 Miss S. M. Armstrong (G.B.)	1969 Miss K. Sawamatsu (Japan)	1983 Miss P. Paradis (France)	1997 Miss C. Black (Zimbabwe)
1956 Miss A. S. Haydon (G.B.)	1970 Miss S. Walsh (U.S.A.)	1984 Miss A. N. Croft (G.B.)	1998 Miss K. Srebotnik (Slovenia)
1957 Miss M. Arnold (U.S.A.)	1971 Miss M. Kroschina (U.S.S.R.)	1985 Miss A. Holikova (Czechoslovakia)	1999 Miss I. Tulyagnova (Uzbekhistan)
1958 Miss S. M. Moore (U.S.A.)	1972 Miss I. Kloss (S.A.)	1986 Miss N. Zvereva (U.S.S.R.)	2000 Miss M. E. Salerni (Argentina)
1959 Miss J. Cross (S.A.)	1973 Miss A. Kiyomura (U.S.A.)	1987 Miss N. Zvereva (U.S.S.R.)	
1960 Miss K. Hantze (U.S.A.)	1974 Miss M. Jausovec (Yugoslavia)	1988 Miss B. Schultz (Netherlands)	

GIRLS' DOUBLES

1982 Miss B. Herr and Miss P. Barg	1987 Miss N. Medvedeva and Miss N. Zvereva	1992 Miss M. Avotins and Miss L. McShea	1997 Miss C. Black and Miss I. Selyutina
1983 Miss P. Fendick and Miss P. Hy	1988 Miss J. A. Faull and Miss R. McQuillan	1993 Miss L. Courtois and Miss N. Feber	1998 Miss E. Dyrberg and Miss J. Kostanic
1984 Miss C. Kuhlman and Miss S. Rehe	1989 Miss J. Capriati and Miss M. McGrath	1994 Miss E. De Villiers and Miss E. E. Jelfs	1999 Miss D. Bedanova and Miss M.E. Salerni
1985 Miss L. Field and Miss J. Thompson	1990 Miss K. Habsudova and Miss A. Strnadova	1995 Miss C. Black and Miss A. Olsza	2000 Miss I. Gaspar and Miss T. Perebiynis
1986 Miss M. Jaggard and Miss L. O'Neill	1991 Miss C. Barclay and Miss L. Zaltz	1996 Miss O. Barabanschikova and Miss A. Mauresmo